afternoon tea parties

afternoon tea parties

SUSANNAH BLAKE
photography by Martin Brigdale

RYLAND
PETERS
& SMALL
LONDON NEW YORK

For the girls!

Designers **Pamela Daniels**
& Megan Smith
Senior editor **Julia Charles**
Production **Hazel Kirkman**
Art director **Leslie Harrington**
Publishing director **Alison Starling**

Prop stylist **Helen Trent**
Food stylists **Bridget Sargeson**
& Linda Tubby
Assistant food stylist **Stella Sargeson**
Indexer **Hilary Bird**

First published in the
United States in 2008
519 Broadway, 5th Floor
New York, NY 10012
www.rylandpeters.com

10 9 8 7 6 5 4 3 2 1

Text © Susannah Blake 2008
Design and commissioned photographs
© Ryland Peters & Small 2008

Library of Congress Cataloging-in-
Publication Data

Blake, Susannah.
  Afternoon tea parties / Susannah Blake ;
photography by Martin Brigdale.
-- 1st ed.
     p. cm.
  Includes index.
  ISBN 978-1-84597-724-5
  1. Afternoon teas. 2. Cookery. I. Title.
TX736.B634 2008
641.5'3--dc22

2008026416

Printed and bound in China.

Author's acknowledgments
Thank you to all my taste-testers for so
happily munching and accepting cakes at
every and any opportunity. But thank you
especially to Julie for advice and inspiration
when it comes to feeding teddy bears, and
to David for always looking so gleeful at the
prospect of another cake.

Contents

Introduction

The custom of afternoon tea is widely credited to Anna, the Duchess of Bedford, the wife of the seventh Duke of Bedford (1788–1861). At a time when meals took the form of a vast breakfast, followed by a light, picnic-style lunch and then a yawning gap until a late dinner in the evening, Anna proclaimed she had a "sinking feeling" in the middle of the afternoon. To remedy this, she ordered cakes and tea at five o'clock. This delightful repast was soon picked up on and ladies would entertain, giving afternoon tea in turn.

The tradition of afternoon tea that we know and love became firmly established by the early nineteenth century, and Mrs Beeton described the meal in 1861 as "...tea and bread and butter, and a few elegant trifles in the way of cake and fruit." Today, afternoon tea appears to be little changed, although perhaps the hotel teas enjoyed in London are somewhat more opulent and decadent than the meal's earlier incarnations. Tea is still served in a pot with milk or lemon, the bread and butter has evolved into dainty finger sandwiches or other savory treats, and the elegant trifles now include scones with cream and jam, delicate sweet cookies, large cakes, and other fancies such as meringues and fruit-filled tartlets.

In today's health-conscious age, where time is of the essence, afternoon tea as a daily occurrence has fallen by the way-side, but it is seeing a resurgence in popularity as a way of entertaining. What could be a more charming and relaxing way to offer hospitality to your friends and loved ones than with a mid-afternoon feast? Taking time out from the hectic pace of life to sit back, relax, chat, and enjoy each other's company? Afternoon tea is a civilized affair, without the stress or expenditure that a grand dinner party can entail. It has all the sophistication of smart entertaining, but in a relaxed environment—a meal of informal elegance that can be enjoyed in the cozy, relaxed environment of your living room or garden.

For this book, I have created twenty different tea party menus, each with their own distinctive character and charm. The menus draw not only on the traditional English afternoon tea, but look more widely to other tea traditions around the world—the Japanese tea ceremony that is so central to the Japanese culture and way of life, the Russian tea ceremony, Moroccan mint tea, and of course that classic summertime refresher in the southern United States, iced tea. Each tea is a unique and individual affair, with a specific focus that means each menu will suit a different occasion, whether it's a tea party in the garden on a sunny afternoon, a birthday celebration for children or adults, a romantic tea for two, or a tea to enjoy in front of a roaring fire on a dark and wintry day. Whichever tea party you choose, approach it with a sense of fun and *joie de vivre*—after all, it is a lighthearted meal and a frivolous decadence to be enjoyed with your dearest friends and loved ones.

Classic English Tea

Darjeeling

finger sandwiches

scones with cream and jam

butter cookies

lemon drizzle cake

That wonderful ritual of afternoon tea can take so many shapes and forms, but the old-fashioned English tea—starting with finger sandwiches and followed by scones spread with homemade jam and whipped cream, golden, crumbly cookies, and a mouthwatering slice of buttery, freshly baked cake—is hard to beat. The menu for this classic tea draws on the absolute best of the afternoon tea tradition, selecting the simplest, most delicious recipes to recreate the quintessential English teatime experience.

finger sandwiches
Makes 12–16

A plateful of dainty little finger sandwiches, each one just a few mouthfuls, is the only way to begin a traditional afternoon tea. Classic fillings include thinly sliced cucumber or wafer-thin smoked salmon, but for a more sophisticated feel, try these irresistible fillings.

8 slices white or whole-wheat bread
butter, at room temperature, for
   spreading

FOR THE SHRIMP IN LEMON AND
CHILI MAYONNAISE WITH ARUGULA
2 tablespoons mayonnaise
1½ teaspoons sweet chili sauce
1 teaspoon finely grated lemon peel
6 oz. cooked, peeled small shrimp
a handful of arugula

FOR THE ARTICHOKE PÂTÉ WITH
HALF-DRIED TOMATOES
14 oz. jar artichokes, drained
½ garlic clove
½ teaspoon ground coriander
1 tablespoon olive oil
3 oz. half-dried tomatoes
a few fresh basil leaves, roughly torn
freshly ground black pepper

To make the shrimp sandwiches, put the mayonnaise, sweet chili sauce, and lemon peel in a bowl and stir to combine. Add the shrimp and gently fold together.

Thinly butter four slices of bread. Spread the shrimp mixture on top of two of the slices, top with arugula and lay the other two slices of bread on top. To cut, put your hand on top of the sandwich and press down gently. Using a serrated knife and a gentle sawing motion, cut off the crusts. Next, cut the sandwich lengthwise into three fingers.

To make the artichoke pâté, put the artichokes, garlic, coriander, and olive oil in a food processor. Add a good grinding of black pepper and whizz until smooth.

Thinly butter the remaining four slices of bread. Spread two slices with the pâté. (Any left over can be stored in the fridge for a couple of days.) Top each sandwich with a few half-dried tomatoes. Sprinkle with basil and top with the remaining slices of bread. Cut as previously described.

DARJEELING
Considered by many to be the "Champagne" of Indian teas, Darjeeling is the classic choice for afternoon tea. It is grown in the foothills of the Himalayas and the First Flush pickings make a light, flowery, and highly aromatic drink that is considered to be among the finest of teas available. Second Flush pickings have a more developed, fruitier flavor, but all Darjeelings are of excellent quality and produce finely flavored tea.

scones with cream and jam

Makes 10–12

Scones are an essential part of an English afternoon tea. They're always at their best when freshly baked and served split open and smothered in thick whipped cream and lashings of homemade jam.

1½ cups self-rising flour
1 teaspoon baking powder
2 tablespoons superfine sugar
3 tablespoons butter
⅓ cup milk
1 egg
whipped cream and strawberry or other fruit
   jam or jelly, to serve
a 1½-inch cookie cutter

Preheat the oven to 425°F. Put the flour, baking powder, and sugar in a food processor and pulse to combine. Add the butter and process for about 20 seconds, until the mixture resembles fine bread crumbs. Tip the mixture into a large bowl and make a well in the center.

Beat together the egg and milk and reserve 1 tablespoon of the mixture. Pour the remaining mixture into the flour and work in using a fork. Turn out on to a floured work surface and knead briefly to make a soft, smooth dough. (Work in a little more flour if the mixture is sticky.)

Pat out the dough to a thickness of about 1 inch and stamp out rounds using a cookie cutter. Put the rounds on the prepared baking sheet, spacing them slightly apart. Brush the rounds with the reserved egg and milk mixture and bake in the oven for about 8 minutes, until they are risen and golden in color.

Transfer to a wire rack and let cool slightly. Serve split open and spread with whipped cream and jam.

butter cookies
Makes about 12

Often it's the simplest recipes that are the best and it's hard to beat these crisp, buttery cookies. If you want a little added indulgence, don't roll the cookie dough in Demerara sugar but leave it plain—then drizzle the baked cookies with lines of chocolate and leave to set before serving.

6 tablespoons butter, at room temperature
3 tablespoons superfine sugar
1 cup all-purpose flour
Demerara (raw cane) sugar, to coat

Afternoon tea is popular with visitors to London's top hotels, where they can enjoy this classic tradition in elegant surroundings.

Put the butter and sugar in a large bowl and beat until pale and creamy. Add the flour and stir, then work the mixture together with your hands to form a soft, smooth dough.

Roll the dough into a log about 5 inches long and 1½ inches in diameter. Sprinkle a layer of Demerara sugar on a piece of waxed paper and roll the dough in the sugar to coat. Wrap the log in plastic wrap and chill for about 30 minutes, until firm. Meanwhile, preheat the oven to 325°F and then grease a baking sheet.

Remove the dough from the fridge, trim off the ends, and cut it into slices approximately ¼ inch thick. Place slightly apart on the prepared baking sheet. Pat the edges of the biscuits into neat rounds or ovals. Bake for about 15 minutes until just beginning to turn brown. Let cool on the baking sheets for a few minutes then transfer to a wire rack.

lemon drizzle cake
Wonderfully old-fashioned and an absolute must for afternoon tea, this cake is drenched in a sharp, zesty syrup that gives it an irresistible tang. It's perfect with a cup of aromatic Darjeeling and refreshingly light in both texture and taste.

1½ sticks butter, at room temperature
¾ cup superfine sugar
3 eggs
grated peel of 1 lemon
1⅓ cups self-rising flour, sifted

FOR THE LEMON SYRUP
grated peel and juice of 1½ lemons
⅔ cup superfine sugar
an 8-inch square cake pan, greased and lined

Preheat the oven to 350°F. Put the butter and sugar in a large bowl and beat until pale and creamy. Beat in the eggs one at a time, then stir in the lemon peel and fold in the flour. Spoon the mixture into the prepared cake pan and level the top. Bake in the preheated oven for about 35 minutes, until the cake has risen and is golden. A skewer inserted in the center should come out clean.

While the cake bakes, make the lemon syrup. Put the lemon juice and sugar in a small saucepan and warm gently, stirring, until the sugar dissolves. Bring to a boil and boil for about 1 minute, then remove from the heat and stir in the grated lemon peel. Set aside until needed.

When the cake is ready, remove it from the oven and prick the top all over using a skewer. Pour the syrup over it and leave the cake to cool in the pan. Carefully unmold to serve.

Japanese Tea

green tea

omelet rolls with
scallions

rice cakes wrapped in
red bean paste

green tea ice cream

When hosting a Japanese-styled tea party, it would be impossible

not to acknowledge the ancient tradition of the tea ceremony,

which is so important to Japanese culture, and the principles

of which should guide this tea party as well. However, it should

also be mentioned that although food is often eaten during the full

Japanese tea ceremony, the tea party I have created here does not

follow the same rules. Everything about this tea party should reflect

the calm, tranquility, and harmonious principles of the traditional tea

ceremony. The omelet rolls and cakes should be arranged beautifully

on platters, the ice cream served in delicate portions, and the tea

served in small tea bowls.

THE JAPANESE TEA CEREMONY

Practiced for hundreds of years, the tea ceremony has been strongly influenced by Zen Buddhism. The ritual interweaves the principles of harmony, respect, purity, and tranquility and offers a quiet interlude when the host and guests may strive for spiritual refreshment and harmony with the universe. A full tea ceremony involves a meal and two types of tea—thick and thin—and can last for up to four hours, but there are other shorter, simpler tea ceremonies as well. During the ceremony, matcha—or powdered green tea—is drunk. Guests kneel on mats facing their host, who carries out a series of ritualistic and prescribed movements such as lighting the charcoal brazier, and whisking the matcha and boiling water in a tea bowl. Each guest drinks from the same tea bowl, carefully wiping the edge of the bowl before passing it to the next guest.

The Japanese discovered the benefits of tea-drinking from the Chinese, the result of contact between Buddhist priests from the two countries.

omelet rolls with scallions
Makes 12

This Japanese-style omelet looks stunning and makes the perfect savory bite to serve before the sweet treats. Although it looks a little fussy to make, it's actually very straightforward. Don't worry if your rolling technique is a little messy—all manner of mistakes can be rectified once the rolled omelet has been compressed inside the sushi-rolling mat.

6 eggs
4 tablespoons thinly sliced scallions,
    plus a few whole to garnish
¼ cup chicken or vegetable broth
2 tablespoons mirin (cooking sake)
1 teaspoon soy sauce
1 tablespoon superfine sugar
salt and freshly ground black pepper
sunflower oil, for greasing
*a sushi-rolling mat covered with
    a sheet of plastic wrap*

Put the eggs, sliced scallions, broth, mirin, soy sauce, and sugar in a bowl. Season with pepper and a pinch of salt and whisk to combine. Divide the mixture between two bowls.

Lightly grease an omelet pan using a piece of paper towel dampened with oil.

Take one of the bowls and pour about one-third of the egg mixture into the pan. Cook until almost set, then carefully roll up the omelet and nudge it to one side on the pan. Pour in half the remaining mixture and cook until almost set, then roll up the rolled omelet inside this fresh omelet and return to the side of the pan. Pour the remaining mixture into the pan and when nearly set, roll up the rolled omelets in it in the same way.

Slide the omelet roll on to the sushi-rolling mat, roll up tightly and let rest for at least 5 minutes. Repeat with the remaining bowl of mixture to make a second omelet roll.

Unroll the sushi mat, trim the ends of the omelet rolls and slice each one into six pieces. To garnish, slice the whole scallions into thin strips. Tie a strip of scallion around each piece of omelet roll. Serve warm or cold, as you prefer.

rice cakes wrapped in red bean paste

Makes 10

The Japanese make many different types of sweet rice cakes, but these, known as "ohagi" are particularly popular and are often served to mark celebrations such as the arrival of new seasons. Although they are not difficult to make, you will need to remember to leave lots of time for soaking the beans and rice.

½ cup dried aduki beans, soaked
   for 4 hours
½ cup superfine sugar
1 cup sushi rice
sea salt
a scrupulously clean kitchen towel

Drain the beans, put them in a saucepan and pour sufficient water over them to cover. Bring to a rapid boil and boil for 10 minutes, then drain and rinse well. Return the beans to the pan, cover in plenty of water and bring to a boil. Reduce the heat and simmer for about 50 minutes until very soft. Add more water during cooking so that the beans are kept covered.

Add the sugar and a pinch of salt and stir to combine, then tip the mixture into a food processor or blender and blend to make a coarse purée, Return to the pan and simmer, stirring, for about 10 minutes or until the paste is thick. Remove from the heat and let cool.

Wash the rice several times until the water appears clear, then drain well and let dry for 1 hour. Put the rice in a pan, pour in 1 cup cold water, cover, and bring to a boil. Reduce the heat and simmer for about 10 minutes, until all the water has been absorbed. Remove from the heat, cover and let stand for 10 minutes.

When the rice is cool enough to handle, shape it into about 10 balls. Soak a kitchen towel in cold water, then wring it out so that it feels damp. Spread about 1½ tablespoons of the bean paste in the center of the cloth and put a rice ball in the center. Gently wrap the paste around the ball. Repeat with the remaining paste and rice balls, putting the paste on a clean bit of cloth each time. Arrange on a plate to serve.

green tea ice cream

Makes about 1 quart

Delicately flavored green tea ice cream is a favorite in Japan and a wonderful treat to serve at a Japanese-style tea party. Serve single, elegant scoops in pretty porcelain Japanese bowls. You can find matcha green tea powder in specialist Asian stores or larger supermarkets, and it is available from many specialty Internet retailers.

3 tablespoons matcha (powdered
   green tea)
3 tablespoons boiling water
1½ cups whole milk
3 egg yolks
1 teaspoon cornstarch
6 tablespoons superfine sugar
1¾ cups heavy cream
an ice cream maker

Whisk together the matcha and boiling water, then transfer to a saucepan and add the milk. Set over medium heat and bring almost to the boil. Remove from the heat and let cool slightly.

Whisk the egg yolks, cornstarch, and sugar until thick and pale, then pour on to the hot milk mixture, whisking constantly. Return the pan to the heat and heat gently, stirring constantly, until thickened.

Pour the custard into a bowl, press plastic wrap over the surface, then let cool. Stir the cream into the custard, then churn in an ice cream maker until thick. Scoop into dishes, or freeze until ready to serve.

Champagne Tea

gunpowder green tea

elegant teatime crostini

orange and almond cake

strawberries and cream
with shortbread biscuits

Just mention bubbles and people's eyes will sparkle in anticipation. A glass of frothy, chilled champagne is a classic addition to the ritual of afternoon tea and brings a sophisticated touch to what is already an elegant treat. Whether you choose non-vintage, vintage, dry, sweet, or pink champagne is up to you, but a glass flute misted with condensation is a must. Strawberries have a natural affinity with champagne, so they are the obvious choice as the grand finale of this light and special menu. You can serve a champagne tea for any special occasion, but I think it's perfect in the summer months, when strawberries are in season and at their fragrant and juicy best.

GUNPOWDER GREEN TEA
Most gunpowder teas are made in Zhejiang province in China. They get their rather curious name from the fact that the tightly rolled "pearls" of dried tea leaves resemble pellets of gunpowder. These little pellets gradually open in hot water to release their warm amber color and produce a light and refreshing tea with a herby flavor. Taken without milk, gunpowder tea is the perfect choice for this champagne tea party, as it will not fight for attention with the wine.

Serve your champagne in a fine, thin flute with a hollow stem or, for a more vintage feel, go for a traditional champagne saucer glass, also known as a coupe.

elegant teatime crostini

Makes 24

These crisp little toasts are very easy to make, yet look very impressive when arranged on a large serving platter. You can toast the bread and make the toppings in advance, then simply assemble the crostini just before serving.

FOR THE CROSTINI TOASTS
1 French-style baguette
olive oil, for brushing

Preheat the oven to 375°F. Cut 24 thin slices of baguette and lightly brush both sides of each one with oil. Arrange on a baking sheet and bake for about 10 minutes, until crisp and golden. Transfer to a wire rack and let cool while you make the toppings.

FOR THE PEA AND PARMESAN TOPPING
2 tablespoons olive oil
2 shallots, finely chopped
1½ cups frozen peas
3 tablespoons dry white wine
dried red pepper flakes, to taste (optional)
sea salt
Parmesan cheese shavings, to serve

Heat the oil in a saucepan set over low heat. Add the shallots and gently sauté for about 3 minutes, until tender and translucent. Add the peas and the wine to the pan. Cover and cook for 3 minutes, until the peas are tender, then tip them into a food processor or blender and whizz until smooth. Transfer to a bowl and season to taste with salt and a pinch of dried pepper flakes, if using.

To assemble the crostini, spoon the pea purée (either cold or warm, as liked) on to 12 crostini toasts, top with Parmesan shavings and serve immediately.

FOR THE SMOKED SALMON TOPPING
3 tablespoons mayonnaise
½ teaspoon finely grated peel from an unwaxed lemon
3–4 drops of Tabasco or other hot sauce, to taste
3½ oz. smoked salmon, cut into 12 strips
½ lemon, for squeezing
freshly ground black pepper
fresh dill sprigs, to garnish

Combine the mayonnaise, lemon peel, and Tabasco. To assemble the crostini, spoon a dollop of the lemon mayonnaise on to 12 crostini toasts. Top with a strip of smoked salmon and squeeze some lemon juice over it. Grind a little black pepper on top, garnish with a sprig of dill and serve immediately.

orange and almond cake
Serves 8

Dense, moist, and zesty, this indulgent cake is perfect for a champagne tea. If you like, you could forego the shortbread biscuits (see right) and simply serve strawberries alongside a slice of this cake with a little dollop of whipped cream.

1 seedless orange
⅓ cup ground almonds
1½ sticks butter, at room temperature
¾ cup plus 2 tablespoons superfine sugar
3 eggs
1⅓ cup self-rising flour
½ teaspoon baking soda
confectioners' sugar, for dusting
*an 8-inch round (and at least 2-inch deep)
   cake pan, lined with parchment paper*

Preheat the oven to 350°F. Finely grate the peel from the orange and set aside. Cut away the white pith from the orange and discard, leaving only the flesh. Put the flesh in a food processor or blender and whizz to make a purée. Add the ground almonds and blend briefly to make a smooth paste. Stir in the grated orange peel and set aside.

Put the butter and sugar in a large bowl and beat until pale and fluffy. Beat in the eggs one at a time. Combine the flour and baking soda, sift into the egg mixture, and fold it in. Add the orange and almond mixture and mix to combine. Spoon the mixture into the prepared cake pan and level the surface. Bake in the preheated oven for about 40 minutes, until the cake has risen and is golden. A skewer inserted in the center should come out clean.

Let rest in the pan for 10 minutes, then turn out on to a wire rack to cool. Dust with confectioners' sugar to serve.

strawberries and cream with shortbread biscuits

Serves 6

Sweet summer strawberries are the perfect partner for a glass of sparkling wine. Serve them with whipped cream and buttery shortbread biscuits for a real treat. Simply pile the strawberries in a bowl and let guests help themselves or, if you want to go for a more sophisticated presentation, serve the strawberries and cream layered between two shortbreads to create an elegant sandwich.

2 pints strawberries, hulled and halved,
   (keep 6 unhulled to garnish)
1 tablespoon superfine sugar
2 tablespoons orange-flavored liqueur,
   such as Grand Marnier
whipped cream, to serve

FOR THE SHORTBREAD BISCUITS
Makes 12
1 stick unsalted butter, at room temperature
5 tablespoons superfine sugar, plus extra for
   sprinkling
1⅓ cups all-purpose flour, sifted
confectioners' sugar, for dusting

Preheat the oven to 340°F and lightly grease a baking sheet.

Put the butter and sugar in a large bowl and beat until pale and creamy. Add the flour and beat well to combine. Lightly knead the mixture until it comes together into a soft dough. Use your hands to shape the dough into a log measuring about 2½–3 inches in diameter. Wrap the log in plastic wrap and chill for about 1–1½ hours until firm.

Put the strawberries in a bowl. Sprinkle with the sugar and add the orange-flavored liqueur. Gently toss; cover and chill until you are ready to serve.

Cut the log into 12 slices, each about 2 inches thick. Arrange them on the prepared baking sheet, sprinkle with a little sugar and bake in the preheated oven for about 14–15 minutes, until pale golden. Let rest on the baking sheet for 2 minutes, then transfer to a wire rack to cool completely.

To assemble, spoon cream on to a biscuit, then top with a few strawberries and a second biscuit. Garnish with an unhulled strawberry half and dust with confectioners' sugar. Repeat to create five more stacks. Serve immediately.

Mother's Day Tea

Earl Grey tea

finger sandwiches

lemon shortbread

Victoria sandwich cake

Although Mother's Day falls on different days in different countries, it's usually celebrated in spring or early summer, so the choice of food for this particular tea party menu reflects this, with light and refreshing flavors. The recipes are also wonderfully simple to follow and could be made by children under supervision, so you're guaranteed a tasty spread that's also as pretty as a picture. Mother's Day is also the perfect excuse to decorate the table with beautiful, fragrant flowers freshly picked from the garden.

EARL GREY TEA

This popular flavored tea is a blend of China black tea and essential oil of bergamot. Various stories have developed over the decades to explain its origin, the most popular being that it was specially blended for Earl Grey (British prime minister from 1830–1834) after a successful diplomatic mission to China. Whatever the origin of this famous blend, it is wonderfully aromatic and has a smoky yet citrusy flavor that is light and refreshing. It is best served black with a slice of lemon.

Breakfast in bed might be the traditional Mother's Day treat, but why not ring the changes and set out an attractive teatime spread on a table decorated with a vase of sweet-smelling flowers.

finger sandwiches

Makes 12–16

Egg mayonnaise with peppery watercress is a classic teatime sandwich filling. Brie and cranberry jelly is less traditional, but no less delicious! For more ideas for fillings, see page 10.

8 slices white or whole-wheat bread
butter, at room temperature, for
    spreading
salt and freshly ground black pepper

FOR THE EGG MAYONNAISE AND
WATERCRESS FILLING
2 tablespoons mayonnaise
½ teaspoon Dijon mustard
2 hard-cooked eggs, cooled
a handful of watercress

FOR THE BRIE AND CRANBERRY
FILLING
4 oz. Brie or Camembert, at room
    temperature
1–1½ tablespoons cranberry jelly

To make the egg sandwiches, thinly butter four slices of bread. Put the mayonnaise and mustard in a small bowl and stir to combine. Peel the eggs, put them in a separate bowl, and mash well with a fork. Add the mayonnaise to the eggs and mash again until the whites have broken up and the mixture is creamy. Season to taste with salt and pepper. Divide the mixture between two slices of bread and spread evenly. Top each with watercress and a second slice of bread. To cut, put your hand on top of the sandwich and press down gently. Using a serrated knife and a gentle sawing motion, cut off the crusts. Cut the sandwich lengthwise into three fingers.

To make the Brie and cranberry sandwiches, thinly butter four slices of bread. Spread two slices with cranberry jelly. Cut the Brie into thin slices and arrange them on top. Season to taste with pepper and top with a slice of bread. Using a serrated knife and a gentle sawing motion, cut off the crusts. Cut the sandwich lengthwise into three fingers.

lemon shortbread

Makes 16

A deliciously buttery shortbread with a tangy, lemony topping.

1⅓ cups all-purpose flour
1 stick butter, diced
¼ cup superfine sugar

FOR THE LEMON TOPPING
2 eggs
3 tablespoons all-purpose flour
grated peel and freshly squeezed
    juice of 1 unwaxed lemon
¼ cup crème fraîche or sour cream
½ cup superfine sugar
lemon slices, to garnish (optional)
an 8-inch square cake pan, lined

Preheat the oven to 350°F. Put the flour and butter in a large bowl and use your fingertips to rub them together until the mixture resembles fine bread crumbs. Add the sugar and work the mixture until it forms a soft, pliable dough. Press into the base of the prepared pan in an even layer, then prick the base all over using a fork. Bake in the preheated oven for 15 minutes, until lightly golden.

Meanwhile, crack one egg into a bowl, add the flour and beat until smooth. Beat in the second egg, then add the lemon peel and juice, crème fraîche, and sugar, and whisk until smooth.

Remove the shortbread from the oven, pour over the lemon mixture, then return it to the oven and bake for a further 10 minutes until the topping has just set. Remove from the oven and let cool completely in the pan before cutting into 16 squares or diamonds, as preferred. Garnish with a slice of fresh lemon as shown, if liked.

Victoria sandwich cake

Serves 8

It's hard to beat a freshly baked, golden, buttery Victoria sponge cake filled with fresh raspberries and cream. If you prefer, you can use other red berries such as strawberries or blueberries, together with the equivalent jelly or jam.

1½ sticks butter, at room temperature
¾ cup plus 2 tablespoons superfine
    sugar
3 eggs
1⅓ cups self-rising flour
3½ tablespoons good-quality
    raspberry jelly or jam
1 cup fresh raspberries
½ cup whipping cream
confectioners' sugar, for dusting
*2 x 8-inch round cake pans, greased
    and base-lined*

Preheat the oven to 350°F.

Put the butter and sugar in a bowl and beat together until pale and fluffy. Beat in the eggs one at a time. Sift in the flour and mix to combine.

Divide the batter between the prepared pans and level the surface using the back of the spoon. Bake in the preheated oven for 20–25 minutes until golden brown and the center of the cake springs back when lightly pressed. Turn the cakes out on to a wire rack, gently peel off the lining paper, and let cool completely.

To serve, spread jelly over one cake and top with raspberries. Whip the cream until it stands in soft peaks, then spread it over the raspberries. Put the second cake on top and dust with confectioners' sugar.

Winter Wonderland

spiced Christmas tea

blue cheese and
pear crostini

white chocolate and
cranberry florentines

spiced star cookies

snow-topped coconut cake

When it's cold and frosty outside and the nights are drawing in,
there's no better time to stay indoors and enjoy a silvery-white winter
tea party. If you are holding it at Christmas you can really go to town
with the decorations—why not dress the table with sprigs of silver
foliage and vases of baubles, and hang sparkly mini lights around the
room to create a fairytale wonderland that both children and adults
will adore? The menu is full of the traditional flavors and warming
spices that we associate with the holiday season, and the gorgeous
star-shaped iced cookies and beautiful snowy-white coconut cake
make a sumptuous teatime display.

spiced Christmas tea
Serves 4

1 orange
1 lemon
4 teaspoons Darjeeling, or other
   lightly flavored tea
1 cinnamon stick
3 cloves
4 juniper berries, lightly crushed
honey, to serve (optional)

Pour a few inches of boiling water into the bottom of a teapot and set it aside to warm. Meanwhile, use a vegetable peeler to pare off a strip of peel from the orange. Next, pare off three strips of peel from the lemon.

Fill the kettle with water and bring to a boil. Meanwhile, drain the water from the teapot and add the tea leaves, cinnamon, cloves, juniper berries, and citrus peel. Pour freshly boiled water in and let infuse for 3–5 minutes until brewed to your taste. Serve sweetened with honey, if liked.

SPICED CHRISTMAS TEA
This delicious, subtly spiced brew is Darjeeling tea flavored with citrus peel, cinnamon, juniper berries, and cloves. Serve it black, sweetened with just a little honey. It makes a lovely non-alcoholic alternative to the mulled red wine that is so popular during the winter months.

Why not host a winter wonderland tea party every year and make it a keenly anticipated festive tradition for your friends or family?

blue cheese and pear crostini

Makes 12

Creamy, piquant Gorgonzola and sweet, juicy pear are a perfect pairing on these crisp, bite-sized crostini.

½ a French baguette
olive oil, for brushing
3½ oz. Gorgonzola cheese
1 pear, peeled, halved, cored and cut into 12 thin wedges
12 walnut halves (optional)

Cut 12 thin slices from the baguette—they should be no more than ½ inch thick. Brush each one with a little oil then toast under a preheated broiler until crisp and golden on both sides. Let cool.

When ready to serve, top each crostini with a pear wedge, a thin slice of Gorgonzola and a walnut half (if using).

white chocolate and cranberry florentines

Makes about 24

Perfect little bites, just the right size for balancing on a saucer!

3 tablespoons butter
¼ cup superfine sugar
3 tablespoons heavy cream
3 tablespoons slivered almonds
½ cup mixed nuts, roughly chopped
4 candied cherries, roughly chopped
¼ cup mixed peel, roughly chopped
2 tablespoons dried cranberries
3 tablespoons all-purpose flour
6½ oz. white chocolate, broken into small pieces
2 baking sheets, lined with parchment paper and greased

Preheat the oven to 250°F. Put the butter, sugar, and cream in a saucepan and set over a low heat. Gently stir until melted, then bring to a boil. Remove from the heat and stir in the nuts, candied cherries, mixed peel, cranberries, and flour and mix to combine. Drop teaspoonfuls of the mixture on the prepared baking sheets, spacing them well apart. Bake in the preheated oven for about 10 minutes until golden, then remove from the oven and gently press the edges, using a palette knife, to form neat rounds. Let cool on the baking sheets for about 10 minutes until firm, then carefully peel off the parchment paper, and transfer the florentines to a wire rack to cool completely.

Put the white chocolate in a heatproof bowl and set it over a pan of simmering water. Stir it as it melts and let cool. Spread the underside of each florentine with a layer of white chocolate, then leave to firm up slightly before using the tines of a fork to make wavy lines in the chocolate. Leave to set.

spiced star cookies

Makes about 30

Nothing says Christmas to me like the smell of these cookies.

1 stick unsalted butter, at room temperature
⅔ cup sugar
½ cup corn syrup
1 egg
1 teaspoon ground ginger
3 cups self-rising flour
¾ cup confectioners' sugar, sifted
4–5 teaspoons freshly squeezed lemon juice
edible silver balls, to decorate
2 baking sheets, lightly greased
star-shaped cookie cutters of various sizes

Put the butter and sugar in a large bowl and beat until light and fluffy. Add the corn syrup, egg, and ginger and beat the mixture again until well combined. Gradually sift in the flour, folding it in as you go. Tip the mixture onto a work surface and knead for about 5 minutes, until smooth. Wrap the dough in plastic wrap and chill for at least 30 minutes.

Preheat the oven to 350°F. Roll out the dough on a lightly floured surface. Use the cookie cutters to stamp out star shapes. Carefully transfer them to the prepared baking sheets. Press together any trimmings and re-roll to make more cookies.

Bake the cookies in the preheated oven for 10–12 minutes, until golden. Transfer them to a wire rack to cool.

Put the confectioners' sugar in a small bowl, add a little lemon juice, and stir until smooth. If the icing is too thick, add a drop more lemon juice. Spoon a little icing into the very center of each cookie and spread it out towards the edges using the tip of the spoon. Sprinkle the icing with silver balls and let set before serving.

snow-topped coconut cake

Serves 6–8

This light, creamy cake has a refreshing kick of lime and makes a pretty alternative to a traditional Christmas cake.

3 tablespoons coconut cream
1 stick plus 5 tablespoons unsalted butter
¾ cup plus 2 tablespoons superfine sugar
3 eggs
1 cup self-rising flour
¼ cup shredded coconut
grated peel of 1 unwaxed lime

FOR THE FROSTING
1 cup cream cheese
½ cup confectioners' icing sugar
1 tablespoon freshly squeezed lime juice
¼ cup coconut curls
2 x 8-inch round cake pans, greased and base-lined

Preheat the oven to 350°F. Put the coconut cream in a bowl and soften with a wooden spoon. Add the butter and sugar and beat together until pale and fluffy. Beat in the eggs, one at a time. Sift in the flour and fold it in, then stir in the shredded coconut and lime peel. Spoon the cake mixture into the pans and level the surface using the back of a spoon. Bake in the preheated oven for 20–25 minutes, until golden brown and a skewer inserted in the center comes out clean. Turn the cakes out on to a wire rack, peel off the lining paper, and let cool.

Beat together the cream cheese, confectioners' sugar, and lime juice. Place one of the cakes on a serving plate. Spread slightly less than half of the frosting on top of the cake, then place the second cake on top. Spread the remaining frosting over it and scatter with coconut curls to finish.

Valentine's Day Tea

jasmine tea

chilled vintage champagne

oysters with red wine and
shallot vinaigrette

spiced sugar palmiers

Valentine meringues

sticky chocolate éclairs

What could be more romantic than tea for two? While the tradition on Valentine's day is often an intimate dinner, a late afternoon tea, prepared with love and served in glorious seclusion in a cushioned salon is a truly thoughtful gesture. Put a bottle of champagne on ice, set the table with candles to provide an atmospheric glow, and fill a vase with scented roses. The menu for this tea is a perfect combination of sensuous indulgence, nostalgic romance, and foodie heaven—all designed to ensure that your lover is left in no doubt at all about how you truly feel.

JASMINE TEA

This sweet, smooth Chinese tea with a delicate floral flavor and aroma is the perfect brew to serve with this luxurious menu. Jasmine flowers are gathered during the day then stored in a cool place until night, when they open and release their powerful scent. The flowers are then layered between the green tea leaves and left to permeate them with their heady aroma. The following morning the spent flowers are removed, leaving only the jasmine-scented tea leaves. Jasmine tea should be enjoyed without milk.

oysters with red wine and shallot vinaigrette
Serves 2

One of life's luxuries, oysters are a sensual pleasure and have been revered as an aphrodisiac for centuries. The age-old rule that oysters should only be bought when there is an "r" in the month means they are the perfect choice for February 14th.

6 fresh oysters, well scrubbed
½ shallot, very finely diced
3 tablespoons red wine vinegar
crushed ice, to serve
an oyster knife (optional)

Wrap a kitchen towel around your hand to protect it, then hold an oyster flat-side up. Slide an oyster knife (or a knife with a short, blunt blade) into the hinge and gently wiggle it back and forth to pry the shell open. Discard the upper shell, then slide the knife under the oyster to release it from the lower shell. Repeat with the remaining oysters. Return them to the lower shells and arrange on a serving plate full of crushed ice. Combine the diced shallot and vinegar in a small bowl, then drizzle a little over each oyster. Serve immediately.

spiced sugar palmiers
Makes 12

Incredibly simple to make and delectable to eat, these light, heart-shaped pastries are perfect for a Valentine's tea.

6 oz. ready-made puff pastry dough, thawed if frozen
2 tablespoons superfine sugar
¼ teaspoon ground cinnamon

Preheat the oven to 400°F. Roll out the pastry on a lightly floured surface to a thickness of about 2 inches. Trim it into a neat 10 x 16 inch rectangle. Combine the sugar and cinnamon and sprinkle three-quarters of it over the pastry in an even layer.

Starting from one short end, roll up the pastry until you reach the middle, then repeat from the other end. Trim the ends neatly, then cut into slices ⅜ inch thick.

Arrange the slices on a lightly greased baking sheet, patting them into shape if necessary. Sprinkle with the remaining cinnamon sugar and bake in the preheated oven for about 12 minutes, until risen and golden. Remove from the oven and transfer to a wire rack to cool completely.

Valentine meringues
Makes about 20

These tiny, pale pink meringues with their melt-in-the-mouth texture are ideal for a Valentine's day tea. Serve them piled up on a plate—just as they are— or sandwich them together with whipped cream.

2 small or 1 large egg white
¼ cup superfine sugar
a few drops of red food coloring
whipped cream, to serve (optional)
2 baking sheets, covered with parchment paper

Preheat the oven to 225°F. Put the egg white in a clean, grease-free bowl and whisk until soft peaks form. Whisk in the sugar, one tablespoon at a time, until the meringue is thick and glossy. Add a few drops of red food coloring with the last tablespoon of sugar to achieve a pretty rose pink.

Dollop teaspoonfuls of the meringue mixture on the prepared baking sheets, spacing them well apart, and bake in the preheated oven for about 1¼ hours until crisp. Turn off the oven and let the meringues cool in the oven. Serve plain or sandwiched together with whipped cream.

Small, bite-size treats that you can eat with your fingers add to the sensuality of this Valentine's tea, making it perfect for a romantic lover's tryst.

sticky chocolate éclairs
Makes about 20

There's something wickedly indulgent about chocolate éclairs and these bite-size ones covered with a rich chocolate sauce and oozing with whipped cream do not disappoint! If you're feeling naughty, don't bother with a fork—just pick them up in your fingers, then lick off the mess!

½ cup plus 1 tablespoon all-purpose flour
¼ cup milk
3 tablespoons chilled butter, diced
a pinch of salt
2 eggs
½ cup heavy cream, whipped
2 baking sheets lined with parchment paper
a piping bag, fitted with a ½-inch tip

FOR THE CHOCOLATE SAUCE
4 oz. semisweet chocolate, chopped
½ cup heavy cream

Preheat the oven to 425°F.

Sift the flour on to a sheet of parchment paper. Put the milk, ¼ cup cold water, butter, and salt into a saucepan and bring to the boil. Let boil for 1 minute then remove from the heat and tip the flour into the pan. Beat until the mixture is just smooth and then return the pan to the heat and cook, stirring constantly, for about 1 minute. Remove the pan from the heat and beat in the eggs, one at a time, until the mixture forms a smooth and glossy paste.

Spoon the mixture into the piping bag and pipe 20 small fingers, each about 2 inches long, on the prepared baking sheets. Bake in the preheated oven for about 12 minutes, until golden. Transfer to a wire rack. Use a sharp knife to cut a slit in the side of each éclair. Let cool completely while you make the chocolate sauce.

Put the chocolate and cream in a bowl set over a pan of gently simmering water and heat gently until the chocolate is almost melted. Stir until melted and the mixture is smooth. Use a teaspoon to gently fill each éclair with a little whipped cream. Spoon some chocolate sauce over each one, and serve as soon as possible.

Baby Shower

linden tree or
rosehip tea

creamy tomato and
mascarpone tartlets with
grilled artichokes

baby boy and girl
flower cookies

spiced carrot and
pistachio cake

white chocolate and
lemon truffle balls

Every expectant mother deserves a baby shower a month or

so before the arrival of her new baby. It's an exciting time, and a

wonderful excuse to bring together all her girlfriends for a last bit

of pampering and indulgence before those sleepless nights begin!

A tea party is the perfect choice for the occasion—easier to work

into your guests' schedules than an evening, especially if they have

small children themselves. Set the table with pastel linens for a

delicate, nursery feel and make sure that the mom-to-be has

a suitably comfortable chair in which to sit, as she opens her gifts

and enjoys being the center of attention.

LINDEN TREE
OR ROSEHIP TEAS

For a baby shower, it is best to choose a caffeine-free tea as so many expectant mothers eliminate or try to cut down on caffeine during pregnancy. That said, certain types of herbal teas are best avoided by pregnant women because of their unwelcome therapeutic qualities. Fruity infusions such as rosehip or refreshing linden tree (tilleul), are safe to drink at any stage during pregnancy, and will complement the foods in this light menu.

baby boy and girl flower cookies
Makes 20

These cute, flower-shaped sugar cookies with pink and blue icing couldn't be simpler to make and taste divine.

1 cup plus 2 tablespoons all-purpose flour
6 tablespoons chilled butter, diced
¼ cup superfine sugar
1 egg yolk
2 baking sheets, lightly greased
a flower-shaped cookie cutter, 2¼ inches in diameter

TO DECORATE
⅔ cup confectioners' sugar, sifted
1 tablespoon freshly squeezed lemon juice
red and blue food coloring

Put the flour and butter in a food processor and process until the mixture resembles fine bread crumbs. Add the sugar and egg yolk and whizz until the mixture starts to comes together. Turn the mixture out on to a clean work surface and knead gently to form a soft dough. Shape the dough into a ball, wrap in plastic wrap, and chill for 30 minutes.

Preheat the oven to 350°F.

Roll out the dough on a lightly floured work surface, to a thickness of about ⅛ inch. Use the cookie cutter to stamp out neat flower shapes, then lift them onto the prepared baking sheets. Re-roll the trimmings to make more cookies.

Bake in the preheated oven for about 12 minutes, until pale golden. Transfer to a wire rack and let cool completely before icing them.

Put the confectioners' sugar in a bowl with the lemon juice and stir until smooth. Spoon half of the icing into a separate bowl. Tint one batch of icing pink with a drop of red food coloring, and add a drop of blue food coloring to the other batch.

Spoon a circle of blue icing in the center of half the flowers, and a circle of pink icing in the center of the remaining flowers. Let set before serving.

creamy tomato and mascarpone tartlets with grilled artichokes

Makes 12

These pretty little tartlets make a lovely savory choice. You can prepare the tartlet cases and filling in advance, then simply assemble the tarts at the last minute. For a winter baby shower, you can serve the tartlets warm by simply warming through the filling before spooning into the freshly baked pastry shells.

FOR THE TARTLET SHELLS
⅔ cup all-purpose flour
2½ tablespoons chilled butter, diced
⅓ cup finely grated Parmesan cheese
a cookie cutter, 2½ inches in diameter
a 12-cup, nonstick, mini tartlet pan

FOR THE FILLING
1½ tablespoons olive oil
1 garlic clove, finely chopped
1 large red bell pepper, seeded and chopped
1½ tablespoons mascarpone cheese
½ teaspoon cider vinegar
½ handful fresh basil leaves, chopped,
    plus a few extra to garnish
2 marinated artichoke hearts, drained
sea salt and freshly ground black pepper

To make the pastry, put the flour, butter, and Parmesan in a food processor and process until the mixture resembles fine breadcrumbs. Gradually add about 1 tablespoon ice water until the mixture comes together. Shape into a ball, wrap in plastic wrap, and chill for 1 hour.

To make the filling, gently fry the garlic and pepper in the oil for 20 minutes until soft, then tip into a food processor and blend until smooth. Transfer the mixture to a bowl, and stir in the mascarpone cheese, vinegar, and chopped basil. Season to taste, cover, and set aside.

Preheat the oven to 350°F. Roll out the pastry on a lightly floured surface and cut out 12 rounds using the cookie cutter. Press the rounds into the tartlet pan and prick the base of each with a fork. Bake the tartlets in the preheated oven for about 12 minutes, until crisp and golden. Transfer to a wire rack to cool.

To serve, cut each artichoke heart into six wedges. Spoon a little red pepper mixture into each tartlet case, top with artichoke, and grind a little black pepper on top to serve.

spiced carrot and pistachio cake

Serves 8

There's something comforting and homey about carrot cake, making it the perfect indulgent centerpiece for this cozy baby shower tea. This one has a lemony cream cheese frosting and a dense, moist crumb.

1½ cups self-rising flour
1 teaspoon baking powder
1 teaspoon ground cinnnamon
½ teaspoon ground ginger
¼ teaspoon freshly grated nutmeg
⅔ cup sunflower oil
3 eggs
1 cup light brown sugar
2 cups grated carrot
grated peel of 1 unwaxed orange
⅓ cup roasted, unsalted pistachio
   nuts, roughly chopped
an 8-inch cake pan, greased and
   lined with parchment paper

FOR THE FROSTING AND TO DECORATE
7 oz. cream cheese
½ cup confectioners' sugar
1½ teaspoons lemon juice
grated peel of 1 lemon
chopped unsalted pistachio nuts
crystallized violet and/or rose petals

Preheat the oven to 350°F.

Sift the flour, baking powder, and spices into a large bowl and make a well in the center. In a separate bowl, beat together the oil, eggs, and sugar. Pour this mixture into the dry ingredients and fold together. Add the grated carrot, orange peel, and nuts and mix. Spoon the mixture into the prepared cake pan, level out the surface and bake in the preheated oven for about 1 hour, or until a skewer inserted in the center comes out clean. Let cool in the pan for 10 minutes, then turn out onto a wire rack to cool.

To make the frosting, beat together the cream cheese, confectioners' sugar, lemon juice, and lemon peel until smooth and creamy. Spread over the cooled cake, then decorate with the pistachios and crystallized petals.

white chocolate and lemon truffle balls

Makes about 14

These buttery truffle balls flavored with lemon peel are a lovely treat. They can be made in advance and chilled until ready to serve.

3½ oz. white chocolate
3 tablespoons butter
2 tablespoons heavy cream
¾ teaspoon grated lemon peel
4 oz. pound cake, finely crumbled
mini muffin or petit four cups

TO DECORATE
2 oz. white chocolate
confectioners' sugar, for dusting

Break the white chocolate into a heatproof bowl, add the butter, and set over a pan of gently simmering water until melted. Remove from the heat, add the cream and continue stirring until the mixture is smooth and creamy. Stir in the lemon peel, followed by the cake crumbs.

Take spoonfuls of the mixture and use your fingers to roll them into walnut-sized balls. Place the balls in the paper cases and chill for at least 2 hours, until firm.

To decorate, melt the remaining chocolate in a bowl over a pan of gently simmering water. Dip a skewer into the melted chocolate and drizzle a zigzag pattern over the truffle balls. Chill until the chocolate has set. Dust with confectioners' sugar just before serving.

French Tea

Formosa oolong tea

mini croque-monsieur

macaroons

raspberry and lemon
Napoleons

strawberry sablés

A French tea party should be the height of sophistication. You may

not have access to a chic boudoir filled with Louis XIV furniture but

you can create a feeling of refinement and elegance by laying out

crisp white linen napkins, beautiful china, and any silverware that

you might have. If you have dainty little cake forks this is the perfect

opportunity to use them. Every morsel of food is presented in

delicate, bite-size portions designed to tantalize, titillate, and flirt

with the taste buds. There should be no slabs of cake or scones

slathered with cream at a French tea party—it's high style,

sophistication, and elegance every step of the way!

FORMOSA OOLONG

Oolong teas are semi-oxidized and vary in style from a light, floral liquor to dark brown leafed teas with an earthier flavor. Formosa oolong comes specifically from Taiwan—formally known as Formosa. The long twisted leaves, which are a mix of brown, black, and dark red with hints of green and silver, brew to make a bright, golden tea. It has a remarkable flavor, reminiscent of fresh peaches and apricots with just a hint of spice and there is no astringency or bitterness. And it is this distinctive and rather sophisticated flavor that seems to make it so perfect for a French-style tea party. Sip it without milk, as you nibble on the tasty French sandwiches and pastries in this menu.

In France, the salon de thé is an institution. Highly skilled pâtissiers are masters of their art, creating breathtaking displays of cakes and macaroons in a myriad of colors.

mini croque-monsieur
Makes 12

Crisp, grilled croque-monsieur sandwiches, oozing with melting Gruyère and ham, are a favorite in French cafés. These amusing miniature versions are the perfect savory to serve at the beginning of a French-style tea party. They're simple to make and you could even prepare them ahead of time, ready to toast when your guests arrive.

a French-style baguette
2 teaspoons Dijon mustard
4 oz. Gruyère cheese, grated
3 oz. prosciutto or other ham
butter, at room temperature
chopped flat-leaf parsley, to garnish
freshly ground black pepper

Cut 24 thin slices of baguette, each about about ¼ inch thick. Spread half the slices with mustard, then top with half the cheese and put a piece of prosciutto on top. Top with the remaining slices of bread.

Preheat the broiler to high. Lightly butter the sandwiches on both sides, then arrange them on a grill pan. Broil until golden, then turn over and broil until just golden on the second side. Sprinkle with the remaining cheese and broil for 1 minute, or until the cheese is melted and bubbling. Sprinkle with parsley and grind some black pepper over them to serve.

macaroons
Makes about 16

Little almond macaroons sandwiched together with fruit jam are a French classic and perfect for this sophisticated tea party. They will leave you plenty of room to indulge in the other delectable morsels on offer.

2 egg whites
1⅓ cups ground almonds
¾ cup confectioners' sugar
blackcurrant jam, to serve
*2 baking sheets, lined with
   parchment paper*
a piping bag

Preheat the oven to 350°F. Put the egg whites in a clean, grease-free bowl and whisk until stiff peaks form. Combine the almonds and confectioners' sugar in a separate bowl, then sift into the egg whites and gently fold together until combined. Spoon the mixture into a piping bag and pipe about 32 1-inch rounds on the prepared baking sheets.

Bake in the preheated oven for about 10 minutes, until a light golden color. Let cool slightly on the baking sheets, then use a palette knife to carefully transfer to a wire rack to cool completely.

To assemble, spread half the macaroons with jam and sandwich them together with the remaining macaroons.

raspberry and lemon Napoleons
Makes 8

For me, nothing beats the experience of breaking through the crisp pastry layers of a Napoleon to reach the sweet cream and fruit layered within. This simplified version of the classic French pastry is quick and easy to put together, yet looks utterly sophisticated and tastes divine.

9 oz. ready-made puff pastry dough,
  thawed if frozen
5 tablespoons lemon curd
1¼ cups crème fraîche or sour cream
14 oz. fresh raspberries
confectioners' sugar, to dust

Preheat the oven to 400°F.

Roll out the pastry to a thickness of ¼ inch, then trim it to a rectangle 12 inches x 6 inches. Slice the dough into 8 squares of equal size and arrange them on a lightly greased baking sheet. Bake in the preheated oven for about 10 minutes, until puffed up and golden. Transfer to a wire rack to cool.

Once cool, use a serrated knife to carefully cut each pastry square in half horizontally to create 16 pieces. When ready to assemble the Napoleons, arrange eight of the pastry rectangles on a serving platter. Fold the lemon curd into the crème fraîche and spread about 2 tablespoons of the lemon cream on top of each one. Top with raspberries and a second pastry rectangle. Dust liberally with confectioners' sugar and serve immediately.

strawberry sablés

Makes about 30 cookies

These very simple almond cookies are a French classic and make a lovely contrast to the creamy indulgence of the Napoleons and the richness of the macaroons. It you prefer, you can simply serve them plain, rather than stacking them with strawberries—but it does add to that lovely feel of French sophistication.

1½ cups all-purpose flour
½ cup ground almonds
a pinch of salt
½ cup confectioners' sugar
1 stick unsalted butter, diced
1 egg plus extra beaten egg for glazing
½ teaspoon pure vanilla extract
1 pint very small strawberries
confectioners' sugar, for dusting
2 baking sheets, lined with parchment paper
a round cookie cutter, 2½ inches in diameter, ideally with fluted edges

Put the flour, almonds, salt, and sugar in a food processor and pulse briefly to combine. Add the butter and pulse until the mixture resembles fine bread crumbs. Beat together the egg and vanilla, then, with the machine still running, add the egg and process until the mixture just starts to come together and form a dough. Shape the dough into a ball, wrap it in plastic wrap and chill for at least 1 hour.

Preheat the oven to 350°F. Roll out the dough on a lightly floured surface to a thickness of about ¼ inch, then use the cookie cutter to stamp out rounds. Re-roll any dough trimmings to make more rounds.

Arrange the rounds of dough on the prepared baking sheets. Prick each one a few times with the tines of a fork, and brush with a little of the beaten egg. Bake in the preheated oven for about 15 minutes, until golden brown. Transfer to a wire rack to cool completely.

When ready to assemble, place three strawberries on half the cookies, then top with the remaining cookies. Dust liberally with confectioners' sugar and serve immediately. Alternatively, serve the strawberries in small glass bowls with the sablés on the side.

Floral Garden Tea

Keemun tea

rosemary scones with
cream cheese and
prosciutto

lavender shortbread

dark chocolate floral cake

meringues with
rosewater cream

Summer afternoons, when gardens are in full bloom, are made for

serving this floral-inspired afternoon tea. Arrange a table and chairs

in a shady area of your garden. If you don't have trees to provide

dappled shade, try setting up a parasol or canopy to protect

your guests from the sun. Relax and enjoy this delicious menu of

rosemary-scented scones, shortbread redolent with the delicate

flavor of lavender, meringues sandwiched with rosewater cream, and

a rich chocolate cake scattered with pretty, crystallized violet petals.

Simply heavenly.

KEEMUN TEA

This classic, black China tea has a lightly scented, almost nutty, smooth flavor with a delicate aroma and natural sweetness. It's light and refreshing, making it perfect for this pretty garden party tea and—depending on the strength of the brew—it is delicious served either black or with milk. My preference is for a lightly brewed cup without milk, to let the subtle floral flavors of the scones, shortbread, and cake shine through.

rosemary scones with cream cheese and prosciutto
Makes 12

Rosemary has a wonderfully intense aroma and flavor. These savory scones are topped with creamy cheese and strips of prosciutto—its saltiness offset by the sweet, juicy grapes. Delicious.

1½ cups self-rising flour
1 teaspoon baking powder
¼ teaspoon salt
2 teaspoons chopped fresh rosemary
3 tablespoons butter
generous ⅓ cup whole milk
1 egg
5½ oz. cream cheese
3 oz. thinly sliced prosciutto
3½ oz. seedless grapes, halved
a cookie cutter, 2 inches in diameter

Preheat the oven to 425°F. Put the flour, baking powder, salt, and rosemary in a food processor and pulse to combine. Add the butter and process for about 20 seconds until the mixture resembles fine bread crumbs. Tip into a large bowl and make a well in the center.

Beat together the egg and milk, then reserve 1 tablespoon of the mixture. Pour the remaining mixture into the flour and work it in using a fork. Turn out on to a floured surface and knead briefly to make a soft, smooth dough. (Work in a little more flour if the mixture is sticky.)

Roll or pat out the dough to a thickness of about 1 inch and stamp out 12 rounds with the cookie cutter. Arrange them on a greased baking sheet, spacing them slightly apart, and brush with the reserved egg and milk mixture. Bake in the preheated oven for about 8 minutes until risen and golden, then transfer to a wire rack to cool. Serve spread with cream cheese and topped with prosciutto and halved grapes.

lavender shortbread
Makes 18

These crisp, buttery shortbreads are subtly scented with the delicate flavor of lavender and have a timeless elegance that makes them absolutely perfect for the traditional garden setting of this tea.

¼ cup sugar, plus extra for sprinkling
⅓ teaspoon dried lavender flowers
scant 1¼ cups all-purpose flour
1 stick unsalted butter, chilled and diced
a few sprigs of fresh lavender, to decorate
  (optional)
a 7-inch square cake pan, greased and lined

Preheat the oven to 325°F. Put the sugar and dried lavender flowers in a food processor and pulse briefly until the flowers are just chopped. Set aside.

Put the flour and butter in a bowl and work together with your fingertips until the mixture resembles fine bread crumbs. Add the lavender and sugar mixture and stir to combine, then use your hands to work the mixture into a dough.

Press the dough into the base of the prepared pan, pressing it flat using the base of a glass. Prick the surface all over using the tines of a fork, then use a sharp knife to score into 18 fingers. Sprinkle the shortbread lightly with sugar, then bake in the preheated oven for about 35–40 minutes, until a pale straw color.

Cut into fingers along the scored lines and let cool in the pan. Decorate with fresh lavender flowers, if using, to serve.

A garden in full bloom on a summer's afternoon is the perfect venue for this delightfully pretty and perfumed tea party.

dark chocolate floral cake

Serves 8–12

A crumbly chocolate cake covered in rich, glossy frosting and decorated with crystallized flower petals makes a stunning centerpiece for this garden tea party. Serve it just as it is, or with chilled whipped cream on the side.

3½ oz. semisweet chocolate
1 stick butter, at room temperature
¾ cup plus 2 tablespoons sugar
2 eggs, separated
1¼ cups self-rising flour
1 tablespoon unsweetened cocoa powder
¼ cup whole milk
an 8-inch springform cake pan, greased and baselined

FROSTING AND TO DECORATE
7 oz. semisweet chocolate, chopped
¾ cup heavy cream
crystallized violets

Preheat the oven to 350°F. Put the chocolate in a heatproof bowl and set over a pan of barely simmering water. Let melt, stirring occasionally, then set aside to cool for about 5 minutes.

Put the butter and sugar in a large bowl and beat to combine, then beat in the egg yolks. Fold in the melted chocolate, then sift in the flour and cocoa powder and mix to combine. Stir in the milk, a little at a time, to loosen the mixture.

In a clean, grease-free bowl, whisk the egg whites until stiff, then fold into the chocolate mixture, about a quarter at a time. Spoon the batter into the prepared pan and bake in the preheated

oven for about 45 minutes, until a skewer inserted in the center comes out clean. Remove from the oven and turn out on to a wire rack to cool completely.

To decorate, put the chocolate in a heatproof bowl, then put the cream in a saucepan and heat until almost boiling. Pour the hot cream over the chocolate and stir until melted. Let cool and thicken for about 10–15 minutes, then spread over the cake, smoothing it over the top and sides with a palette knife. Sprinkle with crystallized violets to decorate and let the frosting set before serving.

meringues with rosewater cream

Makes 8

Crispy, sugary meringues are a classic afternoon tea offering. Served as they are here—with a cream scented with delicately flavored rosewater—they're truly sublime.

2 large egg whites
½ cup superfine sugar
2 baking sheets, lined with parchment paper

FOR THE FILLING AND TO DECORATE
¾ cup heavy cream
1½ tablespoons rosewater
a small handful of clean, fresh rose petals,
   to decorate (optional)

Preheat the oven to 250°F. Put the egg whites in a clean, grease-free bowl and whisk until they form stiff peaks. Whisk in the sugar, one tablespoonful at a time, until the mixture is thick and glossy.

Using two spoons, shape about 16 meringues and place them on the baking sheets. Bake for about 2 hours, until crisp and dry. Let cool on the baking sheets, then carefully peel off the parchment paper.

To serve, whip the cream until it stands in soft peaks, then fold in the rosewater. Sandwich the meringues together with the cream and arrange on a serving plate. Scatter the rose petals, if using, over the meringues to decorate.

Bridal Shower

Nilgiri tea

champagne cocktails

savory toasts

strawberry tartlets

creamy lemon cheesecake

A tea party makes an absolutely perfect gathering for a bridal shower. Make it a sophisticated and indulgent affair by serving sparkling champagne cocktails, elegant bite-size savory toasts, delectable fresh fruit tartlets, and a luxurious, melt-in-the-mouth cheesecake. The bride is the guest of honor and needs her friends to make her feel like a princess. Why not think of this party as a warm-up for the wedding day itself and pay extra special attention to all the details? Select beautiful table linens, glassware, and china, and display the food on cake stands. It's a nice idea for each guest to bring a gift for the bride such as a piece of vintage jewelry, a handkerchief, or a perfume bottle. These can be displayed as part of your décor to create an opulent and feminine atmosphere.

champagne cocktails
Serves 6

This classic champagne cocktail will bring sophistication and sparkle to any bridal shower.

6 white sugar cubes
Angostura Bitters, to taste
brandy, to taste
a bottle of chilled champagne
6 twists of lemon peel, to garnish
6 champagne flutes

Put a sugar cube in the bottom of each glass and add about 3 drops of Angostura Bitters to each. Add a splash of brandy (about 1 teaspoon is fine). Top up with chilled champagne and garnish with a twist of lemon. Serve immediately.

NILGIRI TEA

Some 1,500 miles south of Darjeeling and Assam, India's southern tea plantations stretch through the range of the Nilgiri Hills or "Blue Mountains" that run down the southwestern tip of the country. Most of Nilgiri's teas are used in blends, but more are now being marketed as single-source teas and are well worth trying. They produce a bright and fragrant brew with a delicate, slightly fruity flavor that makes them the perfect choice to complement this menu.

savory toasts

Makes 24 (12 of each topping)

These tasty yet light, bite-size toasts are perfect for whetting the appetite.

2 medium French baguettes
olive oil for brushing

Preheat the broiler to medium. Cut each baguette into about 12 thin slices. Lightly brush with oil, then toast on both sides until crisp and golden. Set aside to cool until needed.

FOR THE CHICKEN TOPPING

2 chicken breasts, cut into bite-size strips
2 tablespoons olive oil, plus extra for brushing
1 garlic clove, crushed
2 tablespoons freshly squeezed lemon juice
6 tablespoons mayonnaise
3 teaspoons capers, finely chopped
a handful of fresh basil leaves, finely chopped, plus extra leaves to garnish
¼–½ teaspoon finely grated lemon peel
sea salt and freshly ground black pepper

FOR THE TUNA TOPPING

6 tablespoons crème fraîche or sour cream
¼ teaspoon smoked paprika
¼ teaspoon ground cumin
½ garlic clove, crushed
½ teaspoon freshly grated lemon peel
½–1 teaspoon freshly squeezed lemon juice
3½ oz. jarred tuna fillet in oil, drained
sea salt
fresh mint leaves, to garnish

To make the grilled chicken topping, arrange the chicken pieces in a shallow bowl. Put the oil, garlic, and lemon juice in a small bowl and whisk to combine. Season with salt and pepper, then pour it over the chicken and toss to coat. Cover and chill. Put the mayonnaise, capers, chopped basil, and lemon peel in a bowl and stir to combine. Season to taste with pepper. Set aside.

Brush a ridged stovetop grill pan with oil and set it over high heat. Add the chicken and cook for about 3 minutes, turning once, until cooked through. Spread 12 of the toasts with the mayonnaise mixture. Top with the chicken, and garnish with basil leaves to serve.

To make the tuna topping, combine the crème fraîche, paprika, cumin, garlic, and lemon peel. Season to taste with lemon juice and add a little salt. Spoon the mixture on to the remaining toasts, top each one with a generous flake of tuna, and garnish with mint leaves to serve.

strawberry tartlets

Makes 12

These pretty little tartlets look impressive but are very easy to make. I cheat and use prepared pastry cream for the filling so that the only cooking that's required is making the crisp almond pastry shells. Tiny wild strawberries are perfect, but if you can't find any, simply use slices of large strawberries.

3 tablespoons ground almonds
⅔ cup all-purpose flour
1 tablespoon sugar
3 tablespoons chilled butter, cubed
generous ⅓ cup prepared pastry cream
7 oz. strawberries
confectioners' sugar, for dusting
a 12-hole mini tartlet pan, greased
a cookie cutter, 2½ inches in diameter

Put the ground almonds, flour, and sugar in a food processor and pulse to combine. Add the butter and pulse again until the mixture resembles fine bread crumbs. With the motor running, gradually add 2 tablespoons water until the mixture comes together to form a dough. Wrap in plastic wrap and chill for at least 30 minutes. Preheat the oven to 375°F. Roll out the pastry thinly and stamp out 12 rounds using the cookie cutter. Press the rounds into the tartlet pan and prick the bases with a fork. Bake for 12 minutes until crisp and golden. Remove from the oven, transfer to a wire rack, and let cool.

To assemble, spoon a little pastry cream into the bottom of each tartlet case, top with a slice of strawberry, and dust with confectioners' sugar to serve.

A bridal shower will become a treasured memory for any bride-to-be, so pay attention to the details and make it a truly special occasion.

creamy lemon cheesecake
Serves 8–12

Nothing beats the satisfaction of a rich, creamy cheesecake, and this zesty one, with a gingersnap crust, is just perfect. There's something about the fluffy white sour cream topping too that makes it look particularly bridal! It's delicious served as it is but, if you want to go the extra mile, serve decorated with generous curls of white chocolate or even fresh white rose petals.

5½ oz. gingersnaps
5 tablespoons butter, melted
14 oz. cream cheese
9 oz. mascarpone cheese
¾ cup sugar
grated peel and juice of 1 lemon
4 large eggs
an 8-inch springform cake pan, greased and tightly wrapped around the outside with a single sheet of foil
a medium roasting pan

FOR THE TOPPING AND DECORATION
¾ cup sour cream
1 tablespoon sugar
¼ teaspoon pure vanilla extract
white chocolate curls or rose petals, to decorate (optional)

Put the gingersnaps in a plastic bag and crush them to fine crumbs using the end of a rolling pin. Add the crumbs to the melted butter and mix well to combine. Tip into the prepared pan, spread out evenly, and then press down firmly with the underside of a glass to create a firm cookie crust. Chill for about 20 minutes.

Preheat the oven to 350°F. Beat together the cream cheese, mascarpone, and sugar, then beat in the lemon peel and juice. Beat in the eggs one at a time. Spoon the mixture over the cookie crust and place the pan in a roasting pan. Pour boiling water around the pan to reach about halfway up the sides. Place the roasting pan in the oven and bake for 45 minutes.

Beat together the sour cream, sugar, and vanilla extract. Spoon the mixture over the top of the cheesecake in an even layer and return it to the oven for a further 15 minutes. Remove from the oven and let cool. Chill for at least 2 hours before serving. Decorate with white chocolate curls or rose petals.

Southern-style Tea

iced tea

topped cornbread toasts

chocolate pecan cookies

angel food cake

Give your guests a true taste of Southern-style hospitality. In the South, iced tea is hugely popular and served poured from pitchers into high-ball glasses or tumblers filled with ice, wedges of lemon, and sprigs of fresh mint. This refreshing alternative to a hot cup of tea is the perfect libation to offer at a tea party on a swelteringly hot and humid summer afternoon. You may not be lucky enough to have a porch or verandah but take to the garden anyway. Throw a white lace cloth over the table and pile up plates of savory toasts, pecan cookies, and a light-as-air angel food cake to welcome your friends.

ICED TEA

Iced tea was invented at the 1904 World's Fair in St Louis, when a merchant of Indian tea was faced with the challenge of selling hot tea to crowds sweltering in the summer heat. In desperation, he poured his tea over ice and the cool, copper-colored beverage was an instant sensation. Every true Southerner has her own special way of making the perfect pitcher and the recipe here is just one way. Let your guests sweeten their tea to taste.

iced tea
Makes 1 quart

5 heaping teaspoons black tea leaves
2 cups boiling water
2 cups cold water

TO SERVE
ice cubes
wedges of unwaxed lemon
mint leaves (optional)
superfine sugar, to taste

Put the tea leaves in a heatproof pitcher or large teapot and pour in the boiling water. Let infuse for about 10 minutes to get a really good, strong brew. Strain into a pitcher and add the cold water, let cool, and then chill. Serve poured over ice with lemon wedges and mint leaves, if using, and add sugar to taste.

topped cornbread toasts
Makes 24

Although cornbread is usually served cut into chunks or wedges, here it's toasted until golden to give a nutty, crispy base for fresh-tasting toppings.

1 lb. cornbread

FOR THE CRAB SALAD TOPPING
6 oz. crabmeat
½ green bell pepper, seeded and diced
1 teaspoon freshly squeezed lemon juice
2 teaspoons olive oil
a good splash of Tabasco sauce
½ garlic clove, finely chopped
1 teaspoon snipped chives

FOR THE AVOCADO SALSA TOPPING
1 ripe avocado, pitted, peeled, and finely diced
2 tomatoes, seeded and finely diced
2 scallions, sliced
1 red chile, seeded and finely chopped
a handful cilantro, chopped
½ lime
sea salt

To make the crab salad, put the crabmeat and bell pepper in a bowl. Put the lemon juice, olive oil, Tabasco, and garlic in a small bowl and whisk to combine. Pour it over the crab and pepper mixture. Sprinkle with chives and toss well to combine. Cover and set aside.

To make the avocado salsa, put the avocado, tomato, scallions, and chile in a bowl. Sprinkle with the cilantro and add a pinch of salt, if liked, then squeeze the lime juice over it and toss gently to combine. Cover and set aside.

Preheat the broiler. Cut the cornbread into 24 squares measuring about 2 x 2 inches and ½ inch thick. Arrange the slices under the hot broiler and toast on both sides until golden brown and crisp.

To assemble the toasts, put spoonfuls of crab salad on to half of the toasts and avocado salsa on the remainder. It's best to serve them immediately, as the toasts will lose their crispness if they are left too long before eating.

chocolate pecan cookies
Makes about 14

Pecans are grown widely across the Southern states, so big, buttery, and crumbly pecan cookies are the obvious choice for this Southern-style tea party. And of course, no cookie is really complete without a generous amount of chunky chocolate chips.

1½ sticks butter, at room temperature
½ cup sugar
1 tablespoon whole milk
1⅓ cups self-rising flour
3½ oz. semisweet chocolate, roughly chopped
scant ½ cup shelled pecans, roughly chopped
14 pecan halves, to decorate
2–3 baking sheets, greased

Preheat the oven to 350°F.

Put the butter and sugar in a bowl and beat together until smooth and creamy, then beat in the milk. Add the flour and mix to make a soft dough, then add the chocolate and chopped pecans.

Drop 14 rounded tablespoonfuls of the mixture on to the baking sheets (spacing them well apart to allow the mixture to spread), and flatten them slightly with the back of the spoon. Press a pecan half into the center of each one.

Bake for 15 minutes, until golden around the edges, then let cool on the sheets for about 5 minutes before transferring to a wire rack to cool completely.

These cookies are best eaten on the day they are baked, but will keep for a few days in an airtight container.

The British may be experts at making and serving a traditional cup of hot tea, but when it comes to iced tea, the Americans definitely have the edge.

angel food cake

Serves 8–12

This classic all-American cake tastes divine served with blueberries or juicy wedges of ripe peach.

¾ cup all-purpose flour
1 generous cup sugar
10 egg whites
1 teaspoon cream of tartar
½ teaspoon pure vanilla extract
a pint of blueberries or 6 ripe peaches,
   to serve (optional)
a tube pan, lightly greased

FOR THE FROSTING
½ cup sugar
2 egg whites
2 teaspoons corn syrup
½ teaspoon pure vanilla extract

Preheat the oven to 350°F.

In a large bowl, sift together the flour and half the sugar three times, until very light. Set aside.

In a separate, grease-free bowl. whisk the egg whites with the cream of tartar until stiff, then gradually whisk in the remaining sugar until the mixture is thick and glossy. Whisk in the vanilla extract.

Sift half the flour and sugar mixture into the egg whites and gently fold in, then sift in the remaining flour and fold in.

Spoon the cake mixture into the prepared tube pan and bake for about 40 minutes, until a skewer inserted into the cake comes out clean. Turn the cake out on to a wire rack and let cool completely before frosting.

To make the frosting, put the sugar in a small saucepan with ¼ cup water and heat, stirring until the sugar dissolves, then boil until the temperature reaches 240°F.

In a clean, grease-free bowl, whisk the egg whites until very stiff, then gradually pour the sugar syrup into the egg whites in a thin stream, whisking constantly until thick and glossy. Whisk in the corn syrup and vanilla extract and continue whisking until the frosting has cooled. Use a palette knife to spread it over the cooled cake. Serve with blueberries or slices of fresh peach, as preferred.

Russian Tea Ceremony

Russian caravan tea

iced lemon vodka

blinis with sour cream
and caviar

hazelnut tea cookies

Russian poppy seed cake

Tea was first introduced to Russia from China in the seventeeth century and is now hugely popular throughout Russian society. Central to the Russian tea ceremony is the samovar—an ornate device that is part-urn and part-teapot. The lower unit is an urn with a faucet in which water is boiled, while on top a teapot rests in which a tea is brewed. This strong, black infusion is then poured and diluted according to taste with water from the urn below. The tea is often served in glasses with ornate metal holders. If you want to host a truly authentic Russian tea ceremony a samovar is a must—they can be rented relatively easily. No Russian party would be complete without vodka, so I've included a lemon-infused one here.

iced lemon vodka
Serves 8

The Russians are renowned for enjoying vodka, their national tipple, at any time of day. The sharp, intensely refreshing flavor goes particularly well with blinis and strong black tea.

freshly squeezed juice of 2 lemons
    plus slices of lemon to serve
¾ cup sugar
½ cup vodka
a resealable bottle or container
8 freezer-frosted shot glasses

Put the lemon juice in a pitcher, add the sugar, and stir until it has dissolved. Add the vodka, transfer the liquid to the bottle, and chill in the freezer. Serve in freezer-frosted shot glasses with small slices of lemon to garnish.

RUSSIAN CARAVAN TEA

This is a blend of black teas from China which has a slightly smoky flavour. It recreates the taste of the teas that were transported back to Moscow from the Chinese border after furs had been traded for tea. Since the journey by camel caravan was long and slow, the traders had to camp. They would stop for the night and light fires to keep warm and cook food. It's believed that the tea absorbed a little smoke from the fires. Today, Russian caravan blends often include a hint of lapsang souchong to achieve a similar effect.

Over the last 200 years, the tea ceremony has become one of the most pervasive cultural traditions in Central Russia.

blinis with sour cream and caviar

Makes about 30

Traditional Russian blinis are made with a yeasted batter, but these are leavened with baking powder and are much quicker to make. They provide the perfect base for the sour cream and salty caviar, which explodes tantalizingly on your tongue.

½ cup all-purpose flour
½ cup buckwheat flour
1 teaspoon baking powder
a good pinch of sea salt
1 egg
¾ cup milk
2 tablespoons butter, melted,
   plus extra for greasing

FOR THE TOPPING
⅓ cup sour cream
½ teaspoon finely grated lemon peel
2–3 tablespoons caviar, salmon roe
   (or roughly chopped smoked
   salmon, if preferred)
freshly ground black pepper

Put the sour cream in a bowl and add the lemon peel. Stir to combine, then cover and store in the fridge until needed.

Set a stovetop grill pan or skillet over low heat. Combine the flours, baking powder, and salt in a bowl and make a well in the center. Beat together the egg, milk, and melted butter, then pour into the well. Gradually work in the flour, using a fork to make a smooth batter.

Lightly grease the stovetop grill pan or skillet with butter, using a paper towel. Drop small spoonfuls of the blini batter into the pan. Cook for about 2 minutes, until bubbles appear on the surface, then flip over and cook for a further minute, or until golden. As you make the blinis, keep them warm in a low oven.

To serve, top each blini with a little sour cream and about ¼ teaspoon of caviar. Grind a little black pepper on top and serve immediately.

hazelnut tea cookies
Makes 12

Frequently referred to as Russian teacakes, these plump, round, sugared cookies look wonderful piled up on a little plate alongside the ubiquitous poppy seed cake. These are made with hazelnuts, but popular variations are made with almonds and walnuts.

5 tablespoons butter, at room
 temperature
3 tablespoons confectioners' sugar,
 sifted, plus extra for rolling
¼ teaspoon pure vanilla extract
⅓ cup finely chopped toasted
 hazelnuts
⅔ cup all-purpose flour

Preheat the oven to 350°F. Put the butter and confectioners' sugar in a bowl and beat until smooth. Add the vanilla extract and hazelnuts and mix to combine. Add the flour and bring the mixture together to make a stiff dough.

With cool hands, roll the dough into 12 balls, each about 1 inch in diameter, and arrange them on a greased baking sheet. Bake for about 12 minutes, until a pale golden color.

Spoon ¼ cup confectioners' sugar into a wide, shallow bowl. While the cookies are still hot from the oven, roll them in the sugar to coat, then transfer to a wire rack to cool. When completely cool, roll in sugar a second time to coat. (Add more sugar to the bowl, if necessary.)

Russian poppy seed cake

Serves 8–12

You will find versions of this classic cake all over Russia, the Ukraine and Eastern Europe. It is delicious eaten with the strong, dark tea favored by Russians. The poppy seeds give it a subtle yet distinctive flavor and striking dark appearance when you cut into it.

¾ cup poppy seeds
⅔ cup milk
1 stick butter, at room temperature
1⅓ cups sugar
1 teaspoon pure vanilla extract
2 eggs, separated
1⅓ cups flour
2 teaspoons baking powder
¼ teaspoon sea salt
confectioners' sugar, for dusting
a 9 x 5 x 3-inch loaf pan, greased and lined with parchment paper

Put the poppy seeds in a food processor or blender and process for about 1 minute, until finely chopped and almost damp-looking in appearance. Tip the seeds into a saucepan, pour in the milk, and bring to a boil, stirring once or twice. Remove from the heat and let sit for about 1 hour.

Preheat the oven to 350°F.

Put the butter and sugar in a bowl and beat until smooth and creamy. Beat in the vanilla extract and egg yolks. Add the poppy seed and milk mixture and mix well until thoroughly combined.

Combine the flour, baking powder, and salt. Sift it into the poppy seed mixture and fold in. Put the egg whites in a separate, grease-free bowl and whisk until stiff, then fold into the cake mixture a few tablespoonfuls at a time. Tip the mixture into the prepared loaf pan and level the surface. Bake for about 1 hour, or until a skewer inserted in the center of the cake comes out clean. Remove from the oven, then lift the cake out of the pan and let cool on a wire rack. Dust liberally with confectioners' sugar to serve.

Gentleman's Tea

Yunnan tea

soft-cooked eggs
with asparagus "dippers"

smoked mackerel pâté
on toast

drop scones
with cinnamon butter

rich fruit cake

This classic tea has a definite air of masculine sophistication about it. Inspired by the unique environment of a traditional gentlemen's club, the menu would be right at home served amidst rustling newspapers and wing-backed leather armchairs. The food is designed to appeal to men's appetites, so it's generous on the savory offerings, with simple drop scones and a rich, old-fashioned fruit cake to follow. Make this wonderful tea as a special treat for any man in your life—husband, father, grandfather, brother, or son—and create the opportunity for him to escape the stresses and strains of daily life and while away a leisurely hour or two over a pot of tea.

soft-cooked eggs with asparagus "dippers"
Serves 2

Although perhaps a slightly unusual choice for an afternoon tea party, soft-cooked eggs are a good accompaniment for the crisp toasts spread with smoked mackerel pâté. Tender asparagus spears are a luxury alternative to "soldiers" and perfect for dipping into runny, golden yolks.

2 eggs
5 oz. fresh asparagus, trimmed
sea salt and freshly ground black
    pepper

Place the eggs in a pan of water and simmer for 3–4 minutes only. Drain and place in egg cups.

Meanwhile, fill a skillet with salted boiling water to a depth of about 1 inch. Add the asparagus and blanch for about 3 minutes, until just tender. Drain well and pat dry on paper towels.

To serve, carefully slice the tops off the eggs. Serve with the asparagus spears on the side for dipping into the yolks and provide little dishes of salt and black pepper to season.

YUNNAN TEA

For a robust menu full of savory and salty flavors such as this one, you need a sturdy tea that can can hold its own. The Yunnan province of China has been producing tea for 1,700 years, and any blend from this region would be a good choice. The tea produces a rich, dark, reddish-black brew with a molasses-like sweetness and malty flavor that's best enjoyed with a little milk.

smoked mackerel pâté on toast

Serves 4

Similar in style to the famous anchovy butter, Gentleman's Relish, this is the ideal way to start this substantial tea. The pâté can be stored in the fridge for up to three days.

7 oz. smoked mackerel fillets, skinned
4 oz. mascarpone cheese
a pinch of freshly grated nutmeg
freshly squeezed juice of ½ lemon
freshly ground black pepper
thin slices of toasted whole-grain bread, to serve

Put the mackerel fillets in a bowl and use a fork to flake them. Transfer to a food processor and add the mascarpone, nutmeg, a little lemon juice, and a good grinding of pepper. Blend to make a smooth pâté, then stir in more lemon juice to taste.

Spoon the pâté into four small ramekins, or a single serving dish, and serve with plenty of hot whole-grain toast.

drop scones with cinnamon butter

Makes about 20

Cinnamon butter is delicious spread on warm drop scones, straight from the skillet. This recipe makes about twice as much butter as you need, so you can keep the rest in the fridge to enjoy another time.

¾ cup self-rising flour
1 tablespoon sugar
1 egg, beaten
scant ⅔ cup whole milk
vegetable oil, for brushing

FOR THE CINNAMON BUTTER
6 tablespoons butter, at room temperature
4 teaspoons confectioners' sugar
½ teaspoon ground cinnamon

To make the cinnamon butter, beat together the butter, confectioners' sugar, and cinnamon until smooth and creamy. Either spoon the butter into a small dish and level the top, or wrap it in plastic wrap and shape into a log that can be chilled until firm and sliced into rounds to serve.

To make the drop scones, put the flour and sugar in a bowl and mix to combine. Make a well in the center. Add the egg and half the milk, and gradually work in the flour to make a smooth batter. Beat in the remaining milk.

Set a large, nonstick skillet over low heat. Brush the hot skillet with oil, then wipe off any excess using paper towels. Drop tablespoonfuls of batter into the skillet and cook for 1–2 minutes, until bubbles appear on the surface. Flip over each drop scone and cook for a further 30 seconds–1 minute until golden. Keep the cooked scones warm as you go. Serve warm with generous pats of the cinnamon butter for spreading.

rich fruit cake

Serves 8–12

This cake improves with keeping so if you can, make it several days beforehand.

1½ sticks butter
½ cup granulated sugar
generous ¼ cup brown sugar
3 eggs
grated peel of 1 unwaxed orange
1¼ cups self-rising flour
1 teaspoon baking powder
2 tablespoons brandy
1⅓ cups mixed dried vine fruits
¼ cup dried figs, chopped
½ cup dried apricots, chopped
¼ cup candied cherries, halved
⅓ cup blanched almonds
a 7-inch cake pan, lined with parchment paper

Preheat the oven to 325°F.

Put the butter and sugar in a bowl and beat until fluffy. Beat in the eggs one at a time. Stir in the orange peel, then sift in the flour and baking powder. Mix well to combine. Stir in the brandy, followed by the fruit.

Tip the mixture into the prepared pan and spread it out evenly. Arrange the almonds on top in concentric circles. Bake for about 1 hour 10 minutes, until a dark, golden color and a skewer inserted in the center comes out clean. Let cool in the pan for about 20 minutes, then turn out on to a wire rack to cool completely. Wrap in foil, and store in an airtight container until ready to slice and serve.

High Tea

Assam tea

smoked trout rarebit

almond biscotti

orange tuiles

coffee and walnut cake

High tea is an old-fashioned tradition. Unlike other afternoon teas, which are served between lunch and the evening meal, high tea is considered much more of a meal in itself. It is often served slightly later than traditional afternoon tea—perhaps at five o'clock or so—and provides an early evening dinner with a more substantial savory (often served hot) than a classic teatime menu. This is, of course, still followed by the usual teatime fancies and a large, indulgent cake. High tea is perfect enjoyed as a pre-theater dinner, when there isn't time for dinner before curtain-up.

smoked trout rarebit
Serves 4

A luxury version of cheese on toast, these hearty rarebits are the ideal high tea savory. Wonderfully comforting, with an oozing, melted topping, they provide just the right combination of indulgence and sustenance.

2 smoked trout fillets, skinned and flaked
4 thick slices of whole-grain bread
6 oz. cheddar or Gruyère, grated
3½ tablespoons dry white wine
¼ small onion, finely chopped
freshly ground black pepper
chopped fresh parsley, to serve

Preheat the broiler. Broil the bread on one side until golden.

Meanwhile, put the cheese and wine in a saucepan and set over low heat. Gently heat, stirring constantly, until melted.

When the bread is golden on one side, turn the slices over and arrange a quarter of the smoked trout on each. Spoon some melted cheese mixture over the top and scatter with some chopped onion. Season with a little black pepper and return to the broiler until golden and bubbling. Sprinkle with a little parsley and serve immediately.

ASSAM TEA
Assam, "the land of the one-horned rhino," is a vast and beautiful area of India, through which the mighty Brahmaputra river runs, carrying rich, fertile soil with it. Assam is the largest tea-growing region in the world, producing 476,000 tons per year. Teas grown here are a distinctive brown color with gold flecks and produce a rich, malty and exquisitely smooth brew that's best drunk with milk.

almond biscotti

Makes about 20

These crunchy finger cookies which snap so enticingly between your teeth, offer a lighter alternative to the other sweet treats on the table at high tea—they are not too sweet, and delightfully nutty.

⅔ cup all-purpose flour
⅔ cup self-rising flour
⅓ cup polenta or fine cornmeal
7 tablespoons sugar
2 eggs
1 teaspoon pure vanilla extract
⅔ cup blanched almonds

Preheat the oven to 325°F. Sift the flours, polenta, and sugar into a large bowl and make a well in the center. Lightly beat the eggs and vanilla extract, then pour into the dry ingredients. Add the almonds and stir together, then knead gently to form a sticky dough.

Use your hands to shape the dough into a flat log about 8 x 4 x 1 inch and place it on a greased baking sheet. Bake for about 30 minutes, until golden.

Remove from the oven and let cool for about 5 minutes, then transfer to a cutting board. Using a serrated knife, gently slice the log into slices ¼ inch thick and arrange them on the baking sheet. Return to the oven and bake for a further 15–20 minutes, until crisp and golden.

Remove from the oven and transfer to a wire rack to cool.

This satisfying tea makes a great choice for a birthday celebration, when a surprise trip to the theater is planned for the evening.

orange tuiles
Makes 14

Delicate, melt-in-the-mouth tuiles are a welcome addition to this menu. Their daintiness makes them perfect if your guests only want a little sweet something to follow the rarebit.

1 egg white
¼ cup superfine sugar
freshly grated peel of 1 unwaxed orange
2 tablespoons butter, melted and cooled
2 tablespoons all-purpose flour
2 baking sheets, lined with parchment paper and lightly greased

Preheat the oven to 375°F. Put the egg white in a large, grease-free bowl and whisk to form stiff peaks. Sprinkle over the sugar and orange peel and fold in. Add half the butter, sift in half the flour, and fold in. Repeat with the remaining butter and flour.

Working in batches, drop 4 teaspoonfuls of the mixture on to one of the prepared baking sheets, spacing them well apart. Spread out into thin rounds using the back of the teaspoon. Repeat with the rest of the mixture. Bake for about 5–6 minutes, until a pale golden color. Let cool for just a few seconds, then carefully remove from the tray using a spatula and drape over a rolling pin to cool. They will become curved as they crisp up. Transfer to a wire rack to cool completely.

coffee and walnut cake
Serves 8–12

This classic teatime cake is enduringly popular, perhaps because something magical happens when coffee and walnuts come together.

1½ sticks butter, at room temperature
generous ¾ cup granulated sugar
3 eggs
generous 1 cup self-rising flour
2 teaspoons instant coffee granules, dissolved in 1 tablespoon hot water
½ cup walnut pieces
2 x 8-inch diameter round cake pans, greased and baselined

FOR THE FROSTING
9 oz. mascarpone cheese
½ cup confectioners' sugar, sifted
1½ teaspoons instant coffee granules, dissolved in 1½ teaspoons hot water
walnut halves, to decorate

Preheat the oven to 350°F.

Put the butter and sugar in a large bowl and cream together until pale and fluffy. Beat in the eggs one at a time. Sift the flour into the butter mixture and stir to combine. Fold in the walnuts and coffee. Divide the batter between the two prepared pans and level out the surface of each.

Bake for 20–25 minutes until golden and the cake springs back when gently pressed or a skewer inserted in the center comes out clean. Transfer to a wire rack, carefully peel off the paper, and let cool completely before frosting.

To make the frosting, beat together the mascarpone, confectioners' sugar and coffee until smooth and creamy. Spread slightly less than half of the frosting over one of the cooled cakes, then place the second cake on top. Spread the remaining frosting over the top and decorate with walnut halves to finish.

Fireside Tea

lapsang souchong tea

warm Parmesan and bacon
pancakes with chive butter

toasted teacakes

sticky marzipan and
cherry loaf

stem ginger cookies

Enjoy this cozy, homey tea in fall and winter when the temperatures

drop and the nights are drawing in earlier each day. Why not enjoy

a bracing afternoon walk in the crisp air to build up an appetite, then

return home to light a fire in the grate, pull up armchairs around the

fire, and snuggle down for tea. The menu, from the pot of smoky,

aromatic tea to the savory pancakes, toasted teacakes, spicy ginger

cookies, and a sticky loaf cake, provides a truly nostalgic and

comforting tea, guaranteed to ward off the winter blues and bring

a warm glow to your guests' cheeks.

LAPSANG SOUCHONG TEA
The distinctive, smoky flavor of this large-leafed black China tea makes it a good choice for a fireside tea—with its delicious, almost tarry fragrance reflecting the warm glow and crackle of logs in the grate. The enticing aroma of the tea is achieved by drying the leaves over pinewood fires, and the best leaves are said to come from the hills in northern Fujian. Lapsang souchong has a golden color when brewed and may be drunk black or with a little milk.

warm parmesan and bacon pancakes with chive butter
Makes about 20

Served warm from the skillet, the combination of bacon pancakes and chive butter is a lovely winter treat and a good way to start this fireside tea.

1 tablespoon vegetable oil, plus extra for brushing
3 strips of bacon, snipped into small pieces, or 2½ oz. pancetta, cubed
¾ cup self-rising flour
1 oz. Parmesan cheese, grated
a pinch of sea salt
1 egg, beaten
scant ⅔ cup whole milk
freshly ground black pepper

FOR THE CHIVE BUTTER
6 tablespoons butter, at room temperature
2–2½ tablespoons snipped chives
freshly ground black pepper

To make the chive butter, put the butter in a bowl and beat in the chives. Season with black pepper. Spoon the mixture into a ramekin or small serving bowl, cover and chill until needed.

Heat the oil a large, nonstick skillet and fry the bacon for about 3 minutes, until crispy. Remove from the skillet and drain off any grease. Wipe the pan with paper towels and set over low heat.

Put the flour, cheese, and salt in a large bowl and season well with pepper. Make a well in the middle. Add the egg and half the milk and gradually work in the flour to make a smooth batter. Beat in the remaining milk to make a smooth batter.

Drop tablespoonfuls of batter into the skillet, sprinkle a little bacon on top, and cook for 1–2 minutes, until bubbles appear on the surface. Flip over and cook for a further 30 seconds–1 minute, until a golden color. Keep warm while you cook the remaining mixture. Serve with the chive butter.

toasted teacakes

Makes 8

There's something particularly comforting and homey about a plateful of freshly toasted teacakes dripping with butter, and the wonderful smell of spices that they always emit. If you've got an old-fashioned toasting fork with a long handle, why not toast the teacakes the traditional way over the open fire.

1½ cups bread flour
½ teaspoon sea salt
1 teaspoon active dry yeast
1½ tablespoons brown sugar
¼ teaspoon freshly grated nutmeg
⅓ cup mixed dried vine fruits
3 tablespoons butter, melted
½ cup whole milk, plus extra
    for brushing
butter, to serve

Sift the flour, salt, yeast, sugar, and nutmeg into a large bowl. Stir in the dried fruits and make a well in the center.

Put the milk and butter into a small saucepan and heat gently together until just warm. Pour into the flour mixture and gradually work together to make a soft dough. Turn out on to a lightly floured work surface and knead for about 5 minutes, until smooth and elastic. Place in a bowl, slip the bowl into a large plastic bag, seal with an elastic band and let rise for 1 hour, until doubled in size. When risen, tip the dough out on to a lightly floured work surface, punch down, and divide into eight pieces of equal size. Shape each one into a ball, flatten slightly, and arrange on a greased baking sheet, spacing slightly apart. Slip the sheet into a large plastic bag and let the dough rise again for 45 minutes, until doubled in size.

Preheat the oven to 400°F. Brush the top of each teacake with milk, then bake for about 15 minutes, until risen and golden and sounds hollow when the base is gently tapped. Transfer to a wire rack to cool. When ready to serve, split, toast on the cut sides, and spread generously with butter.

sticky marzipan and cherry loaf

Serves 8–12

Studded with sweet candied cherries and with a surprise layer of sticky marzipan running through the center, this simple loaf cake will hit the spot.

1½ sticks butter, at room temperature
¾ cup sugar
3 eggs
generous 1 cup self-rising flour
scant 1 cup ground almonds
6 oz. candied cherries, halved
2¾ oz. chilled marzipan, finely grated
confectioners' sugar, for dusting
a 9 x 5 x 3-inch loaf pan, greased and lined with parchment paper

Preheat the oven to 350°F. Put the butter and sugar in a large bowl and beat until pale and creamy. Beat in the eggs one at a time. Sift in the flour and fold in, then stir in the cherries until evenly distributed in the mixture. Spoon half the mixture into the prepared loaf pan and level the surface. Sprinkle with the grated marzipan. Top with the remaining mixture and smooth the surface.

Bake for about 45 minutes, then remove the cake from the oven and cover the top with foil. Return it to the oven and bake for a further 25 minutes, until risen and golden and a skewer inserted in the center of the cake comes out clean. Let the cake cool in the pan for about 10 minutes, then lift out on to a wire rack to cool. Serve the cake slightly warm or at room temperature.

stem ginger cookies

Makes about 10

The spicy and chewy pieces of stem ginger give a kick to these buttery, melt-in-the-mouth cookies which are delicious with a pot of warming lapsang souchong tea. They are the perfect addition to this cozy fireside tea.

6 tablespoons butter, at room temperature
generous ⅓ cup raw cane sugar
1 egg yolk
½ teaspoon ground ginger
2 oz. stem ginger in syrup, chopped
¼ cup ground almonds
¾ cup self-rising flour
2 baking sheets, lined with parchment paper

Preheat the oven to 325°F. Beat the butter and sugar together until pale and creamy, then beat in the egg yolk. Stir in the ground ginger and stem ginger, then the ground almonds. Add the flour and mix well.

Roll the mixture into about ten walnut-size balls and arrange them on the prepared baking sheets, spacing well apart. Flatten slightly with your fingers and bake for about 20 minutes, until a pale golden brown color.

Let the cookies cool on the baking sheets for a few minutes, until slightly firm, then use a spatula to transfer them to a wire rack to cool.

Moroccan Tea

mint tea

toasted flatbreads
with quail's eggs and
toasted cumin seeds

scented butter cookies

gazelle's horns

yogurt and pistachio cake

Hospitality is of the highest importance in Morocco. Even in the

humblest of homes, a visitor will always be offered a steaming

glass of refreshing mint tea, perhaps with some sweetmeats or

fruit. The art of making tea is steeped in ritual, with a great deal of

ceremony in brewing and pouring. The sugar is chipped off a large,

cone-shaped block and added straight to the teapot—usually

a decorative silver one—and the tea is poured into small, ornate

glasses edged with gold. On festive occasions, two teapots, one

for each hand, will be held high above the glasses to create a thick

froth on top. Why not extend some Moroccan-style hospitality to

your friends and invite them to join you for this sensual feast?

mint tea
Serves 4

4 teaspoons Chinese gunpowder tea
 or other green tea
a large handful of fresh mint leaves
sugar, to taste

Pour a little boiling water into
a teapot to warm the pot, then
tip the water away. Add the
tea and mint and fill the pot
with boiling water. Set aside to
infuse for about 5 minutes, then
sweeten to taste with sugar.
Pour into tea glasses to serve.

MOROCCAN MINT TEA

In Morocco, tea is always flavored with fresh mint leaves and
served extremely sweet. Although the making and offering of
tea is now regarded as an institution, it only arrived in North
Africa in 1854 during the Crimean War, when British tea
merchants were hindered by the blockade in the Baltic and
had to seek new markets, such as Tangier, for their imported
China tea. Nowadays, the ubiquitous sweet and refreshing
mint tea of Morocco is the national drink.

toasted flatbreads with quail's eggs and toasted cumin seeds
Makes 12

In Morocco, quail's eggs dipped in toasted cumin seeds and salt are served as a traditional snack or "kemia." I've adapted this idea to create a bite-size teatime savory by serving them on warm, garlicky pita bread with a hint of hot pepper.

12 quail's eggs
1½ teaspoons cumin seeds
2 tablespoons olive oil
2 garlic cloves, finely chopped
3 pita bread
a pinch of crushed red pepper flakes
chopped flatleaf parsley, to serve
sea salt flakes

Put the eggs in a saucepan filled with boiling water and cook for 3–4 minutes. Drain and let cool. Carefully peel and halve.

Meanwhile, toast the cumin seeds in a dry skillet for about 1 minute, until they give off their aroma. Roughly grind in a mortar and pestle and set aside. Heat the oil in a skillet and add the garlic. Fry for just 30 seconds. Remove the oil from the heat and set aside.

Preheat the broiler. Toast the pita breads on both sides, then slice each one into four fingers. Drizzle the garlicky oil over each one, then top with a halved egg. Sprinkle with plenty of toasted cumin seeds, a little red pepper, a pinch of salt flakes, and fresh parsley to serve.

When in season, orange blossom is added to mint tea to give it a refreshing floral lift. In winter, herbs such as sage and thyme, or dried rose and geranium petals might be used.

scented butter cookies

Makes about 16

You will find many variations of these little almond-topped butter cookies all over Morocco. They are often flavored with orange flower water or delicately scented with cinnamon, as here.

1¼ sticks butter, at room temperature
½ cup confectioners' sugar
½ teaspoon ground cinnamon
1⅓ cups all-purpose flour
16 blanched almonds
2 baking sheets, greased

Preheat the oven to 350°F.

Put the butter, sugar, and cinnamon in a bowl and beat until smooth and creamy. Sift in the flour, mix to combine, and bring together until the mixture forms a soft dough.

Break off walnut-size pieces of the dough and roll into balls. Press the balls gently between the palms of your hands to flatten slightly. Arrange the cookies on the baking sheets and press an almond on top of each one to decorate.

Bake for about 17 minutes, until the cookies are a pale golden color. Let cool on the baking sheets for a couple of minutes before transferring to a wire rack to cool completely.

gazelle's horns

Makes 12

These poetically named pastries, filled with almond paste, are a Moroccan specialty and often served with a glass of mint tea. They are flavoured with orange flower water, which you can find in most large supermarkets.

FOR THE PASTRY
generous 1½ cups all-purpose flour
1 egg yolk
¼ cup sunflower oil
5–6 tablespoons cold water
*a cookie cutter, 3½ inches in
   diameter*

FOR THE FILLING
1½ cups ground almonds
½ cup confectioners' sugar, plus extra
   for dusting
2 tablespoons butter, at room
   temperature
1 tablespoon orange flower water,
   plus extra for sprinkling

To make the dough, sift the flour into a large bowl, then add the egg yolk and oil and roughly stir in. Using your fingers, work the ingredients together until thoroughly combined and the mixture is the texture of damp sand. Add sufficient water to make a soft dough. Turn the dough out on to a floured work surface and knead until smooth and pliable. Wrap in plastic wrap then let rest for 30 minutes.

Preheat the oven to 400°F.

To make the filling, put the almonds and sugar in a food processor and process until very finely ground and starting to stick together. Add the butter and orange flower water and blend into a soft paste.

Divide the almond paste into 12 balls of equal size, then roll each ball into a finger about 2½ inches long, with tapering ends.

Using a rolling pin, roll the chilled dough to a thickness of about ½ inch. Use the cookie cutter to stamp out 12 rounds. Place a finger of almond paste in the center of each round and fold the pastry over the top, pressing the dough around the edge to seal. Bend each pastry semi-circle slightly to create a crescent moon shape.

Arrange the crescents on a baking sheet and prick each one with a fork. Bake for about 12–15 minutes, until barely colored. Remove from the oven and transfer to a wire rack to cool.

Sprinkle or brush each one with a little orange flower water and dust liberally with confectioners' sugar to serve.

yogurt and pistachio cake
Serves 8

This light, fluffy cake with a texture similar to cheesecake, is best served cold or chilled.

3 eggs, separated
3 oz. sugar
¼ cup sour cream
1½ tablespoons all-purpose flour
9 oz. Greek yogurt
grated peel and freshly squeezed
    juice of 1 unwaxed lemon
1–2 drops pure vanilla extract
¼ cup pistachio nuts, chopped
a medium ovenproof baking dish
a large roasting pan

Put the egg yolks and 5 tablespoons of the sugar in a large bowl and whisk for a couple of minutes until thick and pale. In a separate bowl, stir together the sour cream and flour until well mixed, then fold in the yogurt, lemon peel and juice, and vanilla extract to taste. Stir this mixture into the whisked egg yolks.

In a separate, large, grease-free bowl, whisk the egg whites until they form stiff peaks, then sprinkle in the remaining sugar and whisk until very stiff and glossy. Add the yogurt and egg yolk mixture and gently fold together. Pour or spoon the mixture into the baking dish.

Place the dish in a roasting pan. Pour in sufficient cold water to reach about halfway up the sides of the dish, then bake for 20 minutes. Carefully slide the pan out of the oven, sprinkle the cake with the nuts and return it to the oven to bake for a further 15–20 minutes, until a golden color and firm to the touch.

Remove the cake from the oven and let cool. Chill in the fridge until ready to serve. This cake is best eaten fresh.

Tropical Tea

tropical tea punch

spicy chicken satay sticks

tropical fruit skewers

wafer-thin spice cookies

pineapple cake with
lime syrup

Bring a taste of the tropics into your home by throwing this zany

tropical tea party. With jewel-bright colors, exotic fruits, fragrant

spices, and fiery flavors to set your taste buds tingling, the menu

will help to transport you to another land. Whether you decide to

throw a garden tea party in the blazing sunshine of summer or bring

a little cheer to a dreary winter's day, this tantalizing flavors on offer

are sure to bring out the feel-good factor in all your guests. To get

the party off to a sizzling start, why not present everyone with a

Hawaiian lei as they arrive?

tropical tea punch
Makes about 5 cups

3 teaspoons black tea leaves, such
   as Keemun or Nilgiri
1–2 tablespoons brown sugar,
   to taste
2⅔ cups unsweetened pineapple
   juice, well chilled
¼ cup white rum
1 lime, sliced
1 orange, sliced
1 star fruit, thinly sliced
ice cubes, to serve

Pour a little hot water into a
large teapot and let warm for
a minute or two. Drain, add
the tea leaves and pour in the
freshly boiled water. Brew for
about 3 minutes.

Strain the tea into a large glass
pitcher and add sugar to taste.
When it has cooled, add the
pineapple juice and rum. Chill
in the fridge. To serve, add the
fruit slices and plenty of ice and
pour into tumblers.

spicy chicken satay sticks
Makes 12

*These classic Southeast Asian
bites, dipped in a spicy peanut
sauce, make a fabulous savory
for serving at this tropical tea
party. You can marinate the
chicken skewers in advance,
then simply pop them under
the broiler to cook when your
guests arrive.*

3 skinless chicken breasts
1 garlic clove, crushed
1 teaspoon grated fresh root ginger
a pinch of crushed red pepper flakes
freshly squeezed juice of 1 lime
1 teaspoon Thai fish sauce
*12 bamboo or wooden skewers,
   soaked in cold water*

FOR THE PEANUT SAUCE
¼ cup coconut milk
5 tablespoons crunchy peanut butter
½ garlic clove, crushed
1 green chile, seeded and finely
   chopped
freshly squeezed juice of ½–1 lime
soy sauce, to taste

Slice each chicken breast into
four long strips and put in a
shallow dish. Whisk together
the garlic, ginger, pepper flakes,
lime juice, and fish sauce and
pour it over the chicken. Stir to
coat, then cover in plastic wrap
and marinate in the fridge for
at least 1 hour.

Preheat the broiler to high.
Thread a strip of chicken on
to each skewer (as shown
above right) and cook for about
3 minutes on each side, until
the chicken is browned and
cooked through.

To make the sauce, put the
coconut milk, peanut butter,
garlic, chile, and juice from
½ a lime in a bowl and whisk
to combine using a fork. Season
with soy sauce and more lime
juice to taste, then spoon into
a small serving bowl. Serve with
the chicken satay, for dipping.

TROPICAL TEA PUNCH
A large pitcher or bowl of
fruity tea punch is a fun
accompaniment to the food
at this colorful tea party.
This refreshing blend of
black leaf tea, pineapple
juice, and rum, garnished
with slices of exotic and
citrus fruit, would be perfect
served in the hazy heat of
a tropical afternoon. If you
want to make this punch for
children, use decaffeinated
tea and leave out the rum.

tropical fruit skewers
Makes 12

Juicy tropical fruits threaded on skewers make a pretty and refreshing palate cleanser between the savory elements and cakes on this menu. You can vary the choice of fruits if you like: papaya or kiwi and star fruit are all good.

3 small ripe mangoes
½ lime
3 bananas
12 oz. lychees, peeled and pitted
fresh mint leaves, to garnish
12 wooden or bamboo skewers

Using a sharp knife, slice the flesh away from each side of the mango pit. Cut each slice in half, then slice the flesh away from the skin and discard the skin. Cut each piece of flesh into three small wedges. Squeeze a little lime juice over each piece.

Peel the bananas and cut them into slices ½ inch thick. Thread pieces of fruit on the skewers and arrange on a serving platter. Garnish with the mint leaves and serve.

wafer-thin spice cookies
Makes 12

Inspired by the flavors of the Indonesian Spice Islands, these giant, wafer-thin cookies are the perfect accompaniment to the fresh fruit skewers. They're so light and crisp that you can just imagine biting into one as you sit on a shady verandah and enjoy the cooling sea breeze.

2½ tablespoons all-purpose flour
¼ teaspoon ground cinnamon
¼ teaspoon freshly grated nutmeg
¼ cup brown sugar
1 egg white
2 tablespoons butter, melted
2 baking sheets, greased
a rolling pin, for shaping cookies

Preheat the oven to 375°F.

Sift the flour, cinnamon, and nutmeg into a bowl and set aside. Break up the brown sugar with a fork, fluffing it up to make sure that there are no lumps, then set aside.

Put the egg white in a separate, grease-free bowl and whisk to form peaks. Sprinkle in about one-third of the sugar and whisk in, then whisk in the remaining two-thirds in the same way. Sift in the flour mixture and drizzle in the butter, then fold together to make a thick, creamy batter.

Working with one baking sheet at a time, drop a small tablespoonful of the batter on to the sheet and spread it out to make an 3-inch round. Repeat to make one or two more

cookies, depending on the size of your baking sheet. Bake for about 5 minutes, until the cookies are browning round the edges.

Remove the baking sheet from the oven and immediately slide a spatula under the cookies, lift them from the sheet, and drape over a rolling pin to cool. They will become curved as they crisp up.

Continue in the same way until all the batter has been used up. (You can prepare one baking sheet of cookies while the other bakes.)

pineapple cake with lime syrup
Serves 8–12

This moist cake, made with brown sugar and drenched with a sweet yet tangy lime syrup, provides a stunning centerpiece for a tropically themed tea. Serve it plain or with a spoonful of whipped cream on the side.

1¼ sticks butter, at room temperature
½ cup light brown sugar
3 eggs
generous 1 cup self-rising flour
½ teaspoon ground ginger
¼ cup crème fraîche or sour cream
8-oz. can pineapple rings, drained and diced
an 8-inch diameter cake pan, lined with parchment paper

FOR THE LIME SYRUP
finely grated peel and freshly squeezed juice
    of 2 unwaxed limes
3 oz. sugar

Preheat the oven to 350°F.

Put the butter and sugar in a bowl and beat until smooth and fluffy. Beat in the eggs one at a time. Sift in the flour and

ginger and stir in, then fold in the crème fraîche followed by the pineapple. Spoon the mixture into the prepared cake pan and level the surface. Bake for about 50 minutes, until risen and golden and a skewer inserted in the center of the cake comes out clean. Turn out on to a wire rack to cool.

To make the syrup, put the lime peel in a saucepan. Add the lime juice and sugar. Heat gently, stirring constantly, until the sugar has dissolved, then bring to a boil. Boil for about 1 minute only, then remove from the heat. Let the syrup cool until it thickens slightly, then pour it over the cake. Let stand for about 30 minutes before serving.

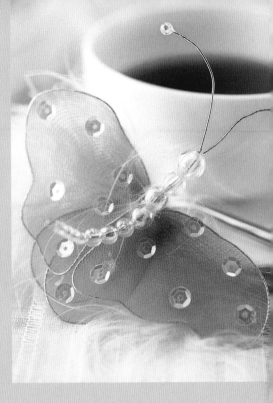

Sweet Sixteen

fruity vanilla "tea"

peanut butter and
jelly sandwiches

love heart sugar cookies

sparkly tiara cupcakes

Any sixteenth birthday celebration should be a fabulously girly affair

and this gorgeous themed party will not disappoint. Don't hold back

on the décor and dress the room with twinkling mini lights, feather

boas, and just about anything that takes your fancy—as long as it's

pink! The food is delightfully, deliciously pretty and the recipes very

simple to follow, so the food can either be prepared ahead of time

or made an integral part of the afternoon—the birthday girl and her

guests can enjoy a girly gossip and a giggle as they bake and

decorate the cookies and cupcakes.

fruity vanilla "tea"
Serves 4

Light, fruity infusions are the ideal vehicle for fragrant vanilla and this lovely tea has just the right blend of sweetness and sophistication for this menu.

1 vanilla bean
4 red berry fruit "tea" bags
  of your choice
honey, to taste

Pour some boiling water into a large teapot and leave it to warm. Meanwhile, fill the kettle with water and set it to boil.

Split the vanilla bean in half lengthwise. When the kettle is coming to a boil, drain the teapot and add the vanilla bean and tea bags. Pour in boiling water and let infuse for about 5 minutes, then pour into cups through a strainer to catch any vanilla seeds. Sweeten to taste with honey.

FRUIT INFUSIONS
A caffeine-free drink is what's needed for this young persons' tea party, so a fruity infusion is the perfect choice. Look out for red berry "teas" such as raspberry, strawberry, or a blend of summer berries with a hint of vanilla. Whatever you choose, make it in a large teapot and serve with a little dish of honey to sweeten.

peanut butter and jelly sandwiches
Makes 12

These cute-as-a-button little sandwiches, with strawberry jelly hearts, are the ultimate in girly kitsch.

6 slices soft white bread
½ cup smooth peanut butter
¼ cup strawberry jelly
a heart-shaped cookie cutter, 1-inch diameter

Lay three slices of bread on a board and score them lightly from corner to corner into quarters. Stamp out a heart shape from the center of each quarter. Set aside.

Spread the remaining three slices of bread with peanut butter, then spread a thinner layer of strawberry jam over the top. Place the slices of bread with hearts stamped out of them on top and pat down gently.

Gently lay your hand on top of the sandwich and using a serrated knife and a gentle sawing motion, cut off the crusts. Cut the sandwiches crosswise into quarters between the hearts. Arrange on a plate to serve.

love heart sugar cookies
Makes about 20

These delicate, buttery sugar cookies are fun to make and look very pretty piled up on a plate on the tea table.

1 stick butter, at room temperature
¼ cup sugar
1 egg yolk
scant 1¼ cups all-purpose flour
2 baking sheets, greased
a heart-shaped cookie cutter, 2½-inch diameter

TO DECORATE
1 tablespoon sugar
red food coloring
2½ oz. white chocolate

Put the butter and sugar in a bowl and beat until pale and creamy. Beat in the egg yolk. Stir in the flour, then knead the mixture gently to make a soft dough. Wrap in plastic wrap and chill for about 30 minutes.

Preheat the oven to 350°F. Gently roll out the dough on a lightly floured surface to a thickness of about ⅛ inch. Stamp out shapes using the cookie cutter and arrange them on the baking sheets. Re-roll the trimmings to cut out more cookies.

Bake for about 10 minutes, until a pale golden color. Let the cookies cool on the baking sheets for a few minutes then transfer to a wire rack to cool.

To decorate, put the sugar in a bowl and add a few drops of food coloring. Work the coloring into the sugar until evenly colored and pink. Melt the chocolate in a heatproof bowl set over a pan of gently simmering water. Drizzle lines of chocolate around the outside edge of each cookie. Sprinkle with pink sugar and let set.

sparkly tiara cupcakes
Makes 12

These are the ultimate cupcakes for princesses everywhere!

1 stick butter, at room temperature
generous ½ cup sugar
2 eggs
¾ cup self-rising flour
1 teaspoon pure vanilla extract
2 tablespoons whole milk
a 12-hole cupcake pan, lined with plain or patterned paper liners

TO DECORATE
1¼ cups confectioners' sugar, sifted
1 egg white
lilac food coloring
about 6 hard red candies
edible sparkles and edible silver balls

Preheat the oven to 350°F. Put the butter and sugar in a large bowl and beat until pale and fluffy. Beat in the eggs, one at a time. Sift over the flour and fold in, then fold in the vanilla extract and milk. Spoon the mixture into the paper liners, then bake for about 17 minutes, until risen and golden and a skewer inserted in the center of a cake comes out clean. Transfer to a wire rack and let cool completely before decorating.

To decorate, leave the candies in their wrappers and tap with a rolling pin to break into large pieces. Set aside. To make the icing, gradually beat the confectioners' sugar into the egg white until smooth and creamy, then beat in a few drops of food coloring until the desired color has been achieved. Spread the icing on top of the cakes. Pile a little heap of candy "jewels" in the center of each cake and sprinkle with edible sparkles and silver balls. Let set slightly before serving.

Big Top Tea

fruity tea punch

"strongman" tuna, corn, and spinach sandwiches

the big dipper

clown cookies

big top cake

Tea parties are great fun for children and this circus-themed party is perfect for a birthday celebration. If you want to go down the costume-party route, invite the children to come dressed as circus characters such as a clown, ringmaster, lion tamer, or strongman. Go to your local party shop and see if they have some circus-themed paper plates, cups, and serviettes. Buy some brightly-colored helium-filled balloons to tie to each child's chair, to create a magical fantasy world in which the children can enjoy their special tea party.

fruity tea punch

Makes 8 small glasses

2 fruit tea bags of your choice
2½ tablespoons sugar
2⅔ cups fresh orange juice
8 oz. strawberries, washed, hulled,
  and thinly sliced

Put the tea bags in a heatproof
pitcher or bowl and pour over
about 2⅔ cups boiling water.
Let infuse for 5 minutes, then
remove the tea bags and stir
in the sugar. Let cool.

When cool, stir in the orange
juice and chill until ready
to serve. To serve, add the
strawberry slices and pour
or ladle into cups or glasses.

FRUITY PUNCH

A caffeine-free fruit infusion makes a great party punch for
a children's tea party. Serve it in a large punch bowl with a
ladle and scoop it into party cups, making sure each child
gets plenty of fresh strawberries.

"strongman" tuna, corn, and spinach sandwiches

Makes 12

These little tuna sandwiches are packed with healthy fresh spinach and guaranteed to build extra-big muscles on little strongmen (and women)!

6½ oz. canned tuna in brine or oil, well drained
2–3 tablespoons mayonnaise
¼ cup canned corn kernels (optional)
butter, for spreading, at room temperature
6 slices whole-grain bread
a handful of baby spinach leaves
freshly ground black pepper

Put the tuna in a bowl and break it up into flakes using a fork. Add the mayonnaise and mix to combine. Add the corn kernels, if using, and season to taste with a little pepper.

Butter the slices of bread, then divide the tuna and corn mixture between three of the slices and spread it evenly over the top. Top each slice with baby spinach leaves and follow with a second slice of bread. Press down gently.

Using a serrated knife, gently slice off the crusts and cut each sandwich into four small triangles. Cover with plastic wrap until ready to serve, to stop the bread from drying out and curling up.

the big dipper

Serves 6–8

Kids love dips and this sweet yet tangy one makes a healthy treat.

½ butternut squash, seeded, peeled, and cut into chunks
2 red bell peppers, cored and chopped
1 tablespoon olive oil
½ garlic clove
1 teaspoon cider vinegar
6 fresh basil leaves, finely chopped
salt and freshly ground black pepper
plain tortilla chips, cucumber sticks, and celery ribs, to serve

Preheat the oven to 375°F. Put the squash and bell pepper in a baking dish, drizzle with ½ tablespoon oil, season, and toss to coat. Roast for about 35 minutes, tossing once or twice, until tender. Set aside to cool.

Put the roasted vegetables in a blender and add the garlic and vinegar. Blend until smooth. Stir in the basil and season to taste. Use a spatula to scrape the dip into a serving bowl. Serve with tortilla chips, cucumber sticks, and celery ribs for dipping.

clown cookies
Makes 12

Funny-faced clowns are always the highlight of any circus. With their big red noses and curly-wurly hair, no one will be able to resist these fun cookies. They may look complicated but are very easy to decorate and children will adore them.

7 tablespoons butter, at room
   temperature
⅓ cup confectioners' sugar
grated peel of ½ unwaxed orange
1 egg yolk
1 cup all-purpose flour
a cookie cutter, 3 inch diameter

TO DECORATE
2 tablespoons butter, at room
   temperature
½ cup confectioners' sugar, sifted
1 teaspoon milk
5 candied cherries, halved
fruit strings in assorted colors,
   or red and black licorice laces
red and black icing writers

Put the butter and sugar in a bowl and beat until smooth and creamy. Beat in the orange peel and egg yolk. Add the flour and mix to make a smooth, soft dough. Wrap in plastic wrap and chill for at least 1 hour.

Preheat the oven to 400°F. Roll out the cookie dough on a lightly floured surface and stamp out rounds using the cookie cutter. Re-roll the trimmings to make more rounds. Place the rounds on a greased baking sheet.

Bake for 10–12 minutes, until a pale golden color around the edges. Let cool on the baking sheet for about 2 minutes, then transfer to a wire rack to cool.

To decorate, beat together the butter, confectioners' sugar and milk until creamy, then use a blob to attach a candied cherry "nose" to the center of each cookie. Spread a little more buttercream along the top edge of each cookie, then twist a strand of fruit string on top to make curly hair, pressing it gently to fix it in place.

Using black icing writers, make two crosses for eyes, then use a red one to draw a mouth. Let the icing set before serving the cookies.

big top cake

Serves 8–12

This cake is incredibly simple to make and decorate, yet creates a stunning centerpiece for a circus-themed tea party. To make it even more special, search out animal-shaped cookies such as tigers, lions, or circus ponies and prop these up around the cake.

1½ sticks butter, at room temperature
¾ cup sugar
3 eggs
generous 1 cup self-rising flour
1½ teaspoons pure vanilla extract

TO DECORATE
4 tablespoons butter, at room
    temperature
1¼ cups confectioners' sugar, sifted
1 tablespoon whole milk
a few drops of pure vanilla extract
5 tablespoons strawberry jelly
about 1 lb. ready-rolled white
    fondant icing
red food coloring
3½ x 1¼-inch piece of colored card
a toothpick
2 x 8-inch diameter round cake pans,
    greased and lined

Preheat the oven to 350°F.

Put the butter and sugar in a bowl and beat until pale and fluffy. Beat in the eggs one at a time. Sift in the flour and mix to thoroughly combine. Stir in the vanilla extract.

Spoon the cake mixture into the prepared pans and level the surface of each. Bake for 20–25 minutes, until golden brown and the cake springs back when pressed lightly with the tips of your fingers. Turn the cakes out on to a wire rack, gently peel off the lining paper and let cool completely.

To decorate, beat the butter until soft, then add the confectioners' sugar, milk, and vanilla extract, and beat until smooth and creamy. Spread a layer of buttercream over the cake, then spread with 3 tablespoons of the jelly. Place the second cake on top and press down very gently.

Trim the fondant icing to a round of about 12 inches in diameter. Force the remaining 2 tablespoons of jelly through a strainer (to remove the seeds) and put it in a saucepan. Add ½ teaspoon water, then warm gently, stirring. Brush the melted jelly over the cake, then gently lay the fondant icing on top, smoothing it down over the top and sides of the cake. Trim off any excess with a sharp knife.

Using a clean paintbrush and the red food coloring, paint red stripes on the fondant icing, starting at the center, to resemble the stripes on a circus "big top" tent.

Fold the piece of card in half and place the toothpick in the fold to make a flag, then use sticky tape to secure it in place. Cut a triangle out of the end of the flag to give pointed ends, then stick the flag in the center of the cake to finish.

Teddy Bear's Picnic

lemon tea punch

baby picnic quiches

gingerbread teddy bears

honey buns

grizzly bear bars

This tea party theme could not be any cuter. You can enjoy an adorable retro children's tea party indoors or out. Create a faux picnic setting indoors by laying out checkered picnic cloths on the floor and setting out picnic hampers full of plates and cups. Invite the children to bring their favorite teddy to sit with them at the party. Alternatively, take the picnic outdoors—either into the garden or to the park or other local beauty spot. Simply pack up the food in a hamper or cooler, pour the punch into a thermos, and set off for some good old-fashioned fun in the fresh air!

baby picnic quiches
Makes 12

Little quiches speckled with sweet onion and bacon are great for picnics. They're perfect to pack in a hamper, and small hands can pick them up easily—children won't be able to resist.

FOR THE PASTRY
⅔ cup all-purpose flour
3 tablespoons chilled butter, diced
1 tablespoon ice water
a cookie cutter, 2½ inch diameter
a 12-hole mini tartlet pan

FOR THE FILLING
1 tablespoon olive oil
¼ small onion
1 slice lean bacon, snipped into
    small pieces
2 tablespoons mascarpone cheese
2 tablespoons heavy cream
1 egg
snipped chives, for sprinkling
sea salt and freshly ground
    black pepper

To make the pastry, put the flour, a pinch of salt, and diced butter in a food processor and process until the mixture resembles fine bread crumbs. Gradually add 1 tablespoon ice water until the mixture comes together. Press into a ball, wrap in plastic wrap and chill for at least 30 minutes.

Preheat the oven to 375°F. Meanwhile, heat the olive oil in a non stick skillet and sauté the onion for about 3 minutes. Add the bacon and fry for a further 3 minutes until cooked and the onion is soft. Combine the

LEMON TEA PUNCH
This refreshing drink is somewhere between a lemon squash, an old-fashioned lemonade, and iced lemon tea and is great for children. Decant it into a thermos for a picnic, or pour into a large ice-filled pitcher to serve at the table.

lemon tea punch
Makes 5 cups

1 large lemon, thinly sliced
4 tablespoons superfine sugar
5 cups boiling water

Put the lemon and any juice in a large bowl and sprinkle the sugar on top. Pour in boiling water and let infuse for about 5 minutes, then strain. Leave to cool, then chill until ready to serve.

mascarpone and cream, then stir in the bacon and onion. Add the egg, a pinch of salt, and a grinding of pepper and mix to combine. Set aside.

Roll out the pastry dough on a lightly floured surface and cut out in to rounds using a cookie cutter. Press the rounds into the tartlet pan and prick the bases with a fork. Bake for about 5 minutes, then remove from the oven and spoon about a tablespoonful of filling into each tart. Sprinkle chives over each one and return them to the oven to bake for a further 15 minutes, until golden and the filling is risen and set.

Remove from the oven and transfer to a wire rack to cool.

gingerbread teddy bears
Makes about 10

Look out for teddy-bear-shaped cookie cutters in kitchen shops. Ready-mixed colored icing sold in squeezy tubes make it easier for small children to help with the decorating.

1 stick butter
2 tablespoons corn syrup
2⅓ cups all-purpose flour
1 teaspoon baking soda
1 teaspoon ground ginger
¾ cup soft brown sugar
1 egg, beaten
teddy bear-shaped cookies cutters in assorted sizes
2 baking sheets, greased
icing tubes in assorted colors and dragées, to decorate

Warm the butter and syrup in a saucepan until melted, then set aside to cool. Combine the flour, baking soda, ginger, and sugar in a bowl. Make a well in the center. Pour in the butter and syrup, add the egg, then mix well to combine. Knead lightly to form a soft dough, then wrap it in plastic wrap and chill for about 20 minutes. Preheat the oven to 375°F. Roll out the dough on a lightly floured surface and stamp out shapes using cookie cutters. Transfer the shapes to the baking sheets and bake for 7–8 minutes, until starting to color around the edges. Let cool on the sheets for about 3 minutes, then transfer to a wire rack to cool completely. Decorate the cookies as desired with icing tubes and dragées.

honey buns

Makes 12

Bears love honey, so they'll love these sticky little honey buns too. Older children will enjoy helping to decorate the cakes in preparation for their teddy bear's picnic, so why not let them help with spooning on the icing and adding the sprinkles.

5 tablespoons butter
¼ cup superfine sugar
4 tablespoons clear honey
⅓ cup whole milk
1 egg, beaten
¾ cup self-rising flour
a 12-hole cupcake pan, lined with paper liners

TO DECORATE
1¾ cups confectioners' sugar, sifted
2 tablespoons freshly squeezed lemon juice
assorted colored sprinkles

Preheat the oven to 325°F.

Put the butter, sugar, and honey in a saucepan and warm gently, stirring constantly, until the butter has melted. Remove the pan from the heat and stir in the milk. Stir in the egg, then sift in the flour and stir in.

Spoon the mixture into the paper liners and bake for about 20 minutes, until golden and risen. Let the cakes cool in the pan for a couple of minutes, then transfer to a wire rack to cool completely.

To decorate, stir the lemon juice into the confectioners' sugar until you have a thick, spoonable consistency. If necessary, add a little more lemon juice. Spoon the icing on to the cakes and finish with coloured sprinkles. Let the icing set before serving.

grizzly bear bars

Makes 14

You'll need big grizzly bear teeth to chew on these delicious nutty and fudgy bars. They're quite rich and sweet so you might want to cut them into smaller squares for very young children.

scant 1¼ cups all-purpose flour
1 stick chilled butter, diced
¼ cup superfine sugar
a 8-inch square cake pan, greased and lined

FOR THE TOPPING
3 tablespoons butter
¼ cup raw cane sugar
14-oz can sweetened condensed milk
⅓ cup hazelnuts
⅓ cup brazil nuts, halved
¼ cup pistachio nuts
2 oz. semisweet chocolate, melted

Preheat the oven to 350°F. Put the flour in a bowl, add the butter and toss to coat in flour, then rub in until the mixture resembles bread crumbs. Add the sugar and stir in, then bring together into a pliable dough. Press the dough into the prepared pan to cover the base, using the back of a spoon to press down and smooth out the surface. Prick the surface all over with a fork and bake for about 25 minutes, until light brown and firm to the touch. Set aside to cool.

While the shortbread is still slightly warm, put the butter, sugar, and condensed milk in a saucepan and heat gently, stirring constantly, until the sugar dissolves. Bring to a boil, then simmer gently over low heat for about 10 minutes, stirring constantly. Remove from the heat, stir in the nuts, then pour the caramel mixture over the shortbread base. Spread out in an even layer and let cool. Drizzle with melted chocolate and let set. Use a knife to slice the shortbread in to bars or squares.

Useful Websites

BAKEWARE AND TABLEWARE

CRATE AND BARREL
www.crateandbarrel.com
Tel: 1–800–967–6696
Carries a wide selection of sleek, modern teapots and stylish tea accessories, as well as an ingenious iced tea pitcher.

WILLIAMS-SONOMA
www.williams-sonoma.com
Tel: 1–877–812–6235
An exclusive assortment of creative bakeware, including cake, cupcake and loaf pans, and a delightful range of cookie cutters, including circus animals and teddy bears.

LA CUISINE
www.lacuisineus.com
A great resource for quality bakeware, including cake pans, mini-muffin pans, and handmade cookie cutters.

THE RUSSIAN SHOP
www.therussianshop.com
Tel: 1–800–778–9404
Visit this website for exquisite Russian filigree tea glass holders, as well as Russian tea blends.

ZAMOURI SPICES
www.zamourispices.com
Tel: 1–866–329–5988
For traditional Moroccan tea glasses in jewel-tone colors (as well as Moroccan mint tea and orange flower water).

INGREDIENTS

WWW.COOLCUPCAKES.COM
Tel: 1–800–797–2887
One-stop store for baking enthusiasts looking for sanding sugar, edible glitter, and sprinkles in a rainbow of colors, plus great paper liners and tiered cake stands, perfect for displaying teatime savories and fancies.

KING ARTHUR FLOUR
www.kingarthurflour.com
Tel: 1–800–827–6836
For decorating sugars, marzipan, candied cherries, and other highest-quality baking ingredients, this website has everything you need.

INTO THE OVEN
www.intotheoven.com
For ready-rolled fondant icing, dragées, sprinkles, edible glitter, and other baking supplies from around the world.

CONFECTIONERY HOUSE
www.confectioneryhouse.com
Tel: 1–518–279–4250
Paper liners in every color, as well as sprinkles and other edible decorations.

WILTON
www.wilton.com
Professional cake decorators know Wilton and baking enthusiasts at every level will enjoy browsing their online store.

KITCHEN KRAFTS
www.kitchenkrafts.com
Tel: 1–800–298–5389
The Foodcrafters' Supply Catalog carries hard-to-find edible dragées, cake stands, fun seasonal paper liners, and food coloring etc.

PENZEY'S SPICES
www.penzeys.com
Tel: 1–800–635–0616
For superb Madagascan vanilla extract and vanilla beans, as well as premium baking spices, visit one of Penzey's retail stores or explore their website.

TEA MERCHANTS

HARNEY & SONS
www.harney.com
These master tea blenders, based in Connecticut, offer an extensive selection of traditional and flavored teas as well as herbal infusions.

UPTON TEA IMPORTS
www.uptontea.com
This tea importer's online store offers over 420 varieties of loose tea and also stocks a wide range of quality teaware.

IMPERIAL TEA COURT
www.imperialtea.com
Tel: 1–800–567–5898
Many of the world's finest, rarest, and most highly acclaimed Chinese and Taiwanese teas available to buy online.

SAMOVAR TEA LOUNGE
www.samovartea.com
Tel: 1–800–415–626–4700
*Teas from small artisans around
the world available to buy
(as well as teapots and sets)
through this San Francisco
tea lounge's online tea store.*

ITO EN
www.itoen.com/estore
*This New York tea shop stocks
a superb collection of specialist
"high-end" Japanese, China,
and Indian teas. Visit their
website to order the most
popular teas, as well as stylish
teapots and accessories.*

TEANOBI
www.teanobi.com
*For Japanese green teas—both
loose and powdered—check
out Teanobi's website. The
name is a fusion of Japanese
and English that translates as
"the beauty or the art of tea."*

TEAS ETC.
www.teasetc.com
*Visit this online store for
loose teas and fine teaware.
Highlights from their wide
selection of black teas include
Darjeeling First Flush, Assam
Reserve, Nilgiri Organic, and
Keemun Mao Feng.*

T'S TASTING BOUTIQUE
www.tealeaves.com
*This Vancouver teashop offers
over 100 unique blends of tea
as well as great accessories.*

Conversion Charts

Weights and measures have been rounded up or down slightly to make measuring easier.

The recipes in this book require the following conversions:

American	Metric	Imperial
6 tbsp	85 g	3 oz.
7 tbsp	100 g	3½ oz.
1 stick	115 g	4 oz.

Volume equivalents:

American	Metric	Imperial
1 teaspoon	5 ml	
1 tablespoon	15 ml	
¼ cup	60 ml	2 fl. oz.
⅓ cup	75 ml	2½ fl. oz.
½ cup	125 ml	4 fl. oz.
⅔ cup	150 ml	5 fl. oz. (¼ pint)
¾ cup	175 ml	6 fl. oz.
1 cup	250 ml	8 fl. oz.

Weight equivalents:

Imperial	Metric
1 oz.	30 g
2 oz.	55 g
3 oz.	85 g
3½ oz.	100 g
4 oz.	115 g
6 oz.	175 g
8 oz. (½ lb.)	225 g
9 oz.	250 g
10 oz.	280 g
12 oz.	350 g
13 oz.	375 g
14 oz.	400 g
15 oz.	425 g
16 oz. (1 lb.)	450 g

Measurements:

Inches	cm
¼ inch	5 mm
½ inch	1 cm
1 inch	2.5 cm
2 inches	5 cm
3 inches	7 cm
4 inches	10 cm
5 inches	12 cm
6 inches	15 cm
7 inches	18 cm
8 inches	20 cm
9 inches	23 cm
10 inches	25 cm
11 inches	28 cm
12 inches	30 cm

Oven temperatures:

120°C	(250°F)	Gas ½
140°C	(275°F)	Gas 1
150°C	(300°F)	Gas 2
170°C	(325°F)	Gas 3
180°C	(350°F)	Gas 4
190°C	(375°F)	Gas 5
200°C	(400°F)	Gas 6
220°C	(425°F)	Gas 7

Measuring butter:
A US stick of butter weighs 4 oz. which is approximately 115 g or 8 tablespoons.

Index

Credits

The publisher would like to thank Farley Prop Hire for use of locations for the following stories:

Bridal Shower (page 66-73), French Tea (page 52–57), Southern-style Tea (page 74–79), and Big Top Tea (page 128–133).

Contact them on + 44 (020) 8749 9925 or visit www.farley.co.uk for further information

Image for endpapers taken from Weaving Patterns published by The Pepin Press www.pepinpress.com